I SURVIVED

LISA M. SOBRY

All poetry copyright © 2007 by Lisa M. Sobry

I Survived Revised Edition 2013 copyright © 2013 Lisa M. Sobry. All rights reserved.

No part of this book may be used or reproduced in any manner whatsoever without written permission from the author except in the case of brief quotations embodied in critical articles and reviews.

This book is dedicated to women around the world who've been abused mentally, physically, spiritually, and emotionally.

You will survive if you choose to.

Thank you so much to my children for loving me, being strong, and supporting me during the process of writing this book.

TABLE OF CONTENTS

Preface	8
Introduction	10
The Early Years	11
Moving to the Farm	14
The Dating Years	18
Douglas	21
Winnipeg	25
Our New Home	28
Struggling with Emotions	31
The Marriage	35
Brandon	42
Vance	45
Charles	49
My Brothers	52
Patrick	58
The Breaking Point	62
On the Road	65
Jack	69
My House	71
My Spiritual Journey	79
Tasha	82

Computer Dating	87
Michael	91
Back to School	94
Marcel	104
My Mother	113
Serenity Oasis	116
What I've Learned	120
Resources	127
About the Author	132

This is a true story.
Some of the names and the places in this
book have been changed to protect
the privacy of those involved.

PREFACE

This book was written to support all abused women. You're not alone, and regardless of where you are in your life right at this moment, I want you to know this: *You will survive*! No matter what happens in your life, *you will survive*! You just need to believe in yourself, know you are worthy, and know you deserve to be happy.

Regardless of what people say or tell you, any type of abuse *is not your fault*. You didn't do anything wrong to deserve the abuse you received.

I'm not an expert and I don't pretend to be. This is the story of my life, how I survived abuse, the life I led because of the abuse, and how I've progressed to where I am today. My hope is that once you've read my story, you will have the tools you need to make changes, to move on, and to lead a happy, healthy life.

If you want to heal, move forward, and live what's considered to be a "normal life," this will help you. It's the story of the journey of my life from my childhood to present day. It may make you laugh one minute, cry the next, and wonder where on earth I got the strength to keep on living. If you're not ready to start a new life, put this book down. Only read it when you are ready to move forward.

Now, let's sit down, and I'll tell you the story of my life. You may want to have a box of tissues nearby. Be prepared for graphic content and any images that may form in your mind.

This book is not recommended for children under the age of 18.

INTRODUCTION

My family lived on a farm in a small community on the Canadian prairies. We were raised with strong Catholic beliefs and attended church every Sunday. After church, we went home, changed our clothes, and went to work on the farm; so much for Sunday being a day of rest.

I don't know very much about my parents' histories other than they both came from farming backgrounds. My father lived on a farm, was raised Catholic, and attended church every Sunday with his family. I've heard bits of information about my grandmother being a manic depressant and abusing alcohol. My grandfather was a gentle-minded soul who believed strongly in the saying, "You made your bed, now lie in it." My mother was raised on a farm, attended the United Church of Canada, and converted to Catholicism when she and my father were married. My grandfather on my mother's side was an alcoholic and my grandmother played the piano.

We were the perfect image of a normal family because all our secrets were well hidden at home.

THE EARLY YEARS

Where to start? For most of my childhood, I was in trouble for one reason or another. My father had a very bad temper and he yelled at me and hit me almost daily. I always felt I wasn't good enough. I was too slow, too fast, not smart enough, or not strong enough. I thought it was because I was the oldest of four children. I've heard the oldest child has to break in the parents before the rest of the children come along. I'm not sure if this is a direct quote from somewhere, or just coffee shop talk; however, I believe it to be true. I also believe that people are supposed to have happy childhood memories, such as sitting on swings, playing games, and laughing at rain drops touching their tongues. I remember one happy memory making homemade ice cream on the front step with my sister when I was 4 years old. I'm sure there are more, but it's the unhappy childhood memories that stand out.

I remember my parents building a house and my being out picking up sticks and roots everyday to clear the yard. Next door to us was a school, but I wasn't allowed to use the playground because I had work to do.

I know part of my father's frustration with me was due to my tiny little bladder. As a child, until I was 12 years old, I remember peeing my pants almost daily. When my body decided it had to go pee, it decided right then. So, I had about five minutes that I could hold it before I could feel my teeth floating. I remember running to the house one time because I really had to go, and my father caught up with me in the carport. He picked me up, put me against the wall, and started yelling at me. I, of course, started crying, and wet my pants on the spot. I honestly thought at that moment I was going to die. My father was so angry and dished out the legendary you-won't-be-able-to-sit-down-for-a-week spanking.

So off I toddled into the house to get changed, and then face my mother. My mother was never as severe as my father was, but she was angry just the same. She never hit me. Instead she would tell my father what I'd done, and he'd be the one to hit me. "More laundry, and why can't you make it to the washroom on time? What's wrong with you?!"

As an adult, I understand it's the way my body is made, but as a child, it felt like the end of the world. What was wrong with me? From the age of four, I had the feeling something was wrong with me that needed to be fixed. No wonder I had self-esteem issues as an adult.

MOVING TO THE FARM

When I was six years old, my parents bought a farm and the work began. My sister and I used to sit on the front of the tractor bucket and every time it stopped, we would grab a stone, or stick, or whatever was there for us to pick up. When we baled, we stood on the rack, pulled the bales off, and dragged them to the back until the hay rack floor was full, and then some. My father would stop the tractor, stack the bales, and away we'd go again. Eventually my parents switched over to round bales, but that wasn't until I was about 12 years old. So the years passed with my either going to school, or working hard on the farm.

Around the age of 10, the sexual abuse started. I was classified as an "early bloomer" in Grade 5. As if the girls and boys teasing me at school wasn't enough, I had to suffer the abuse at home as well.

My family had expanded by adding two little brothers. My sister spent a great deal of time helping my mother inside the house and in the garden. I was the oldest, so I'd be outside on the farm helping my father. It was the perfect opportunity for an abuser; no one watching his every move, my mother busy in the house with my siblings, and so much work to be done that required me being outside for long periods of time with him.

The pattern was always the same. I would come home from school, change into old clothes, and then head outside to help my father. Ninety-nine percent of the time, the first thing he did when he saw me was grab my breasts. He'd play with my nipples and say how much my mother hated that. Then he'd kiss me and hug me like an adult. I would cry and cry and cry. This happened every day; I honestly can't remember a day going by when I wasn't touched in some way. I'd tried to think of other places I could be in my mind, but my father would always bring me back to the moment, telling me how much he liked it and asking didn't it feel good.

I used to pray my parents would get a divorce and I would go live with my mother. When I went to church, I would go to confession, confess my sins (usually swearing at my siblings), then go back to the pew, and pray my heart out. I still have issues with God and my mother for not stopping my father from abusing me.

The older I grew and the more I developed, the more the abuse escalated. I begged my mother not to make me shower with my father, but the response was always, "We have to conserve water, you know." During those showers, I was forced to practice "milking the cow." As a child, I didn't understand why my father's penis grew hard when I practiced pulling gently on his balls one at a time as if I was milking a cow. I was told this was to improve my wrists and fingers, so it would be easier for me to milk our two cows. He would also fondle my breasts and kiss me like an adult with his tongue. I would cry and cry. As an adult, it disgusts me that a father could take advantage of a child like that, and that a mother would not stop it.

She knew. My mother knew, that is. She even caught him a couple of times when he was touching my breasts. My shirt was lifted up, bra undone, and he was squeezing and playing with them. I was crying. She asked him, "What the hell is going on?" He'd just walked away. Then she turned on me with questions that just made me out to be the bad person. My father was never to blame! "How can you allow him to do that?" "Why didn't you tell me?" "Why don't you stop him?" "Do you like it?" My response was always the same, "I told you I didn't want to be left alone with him. I told you I didn't want to have showers with him. Every time you catch him, or I tell you, he just touches me twice as much as he did before, and you don't stop him. I can't stop him, you have to! And NO, I hate it; I have never liked it and never will. You know he does it, you see me crying all the time, and YOU still don't stop him!"

So it continued. He was angry whenever he got caught, so he took it out on me. A piece of machinery would break, and I would get hit for it because it was my fault. I was not strong enough to lift something, so I got cursed at and hit because of it. I talked back to my mother, so I got a spanking. I'm not talking about a tap-on-the-butt spanking. I'm talking about a leather belt, so you-can't-sit-down-for-a-week-afterwards spanking. In addition, I'd have to take off all my clothes, sit on his lap, and let him molest me for half an hour until he was satisfied. Only then could I bend over the bed and get hit over and over again until he felt I've learned my lesson.

Where was my mother during these obscene spankings? Upstairs.

THE DATING YEARS

At the age of 14, I started dating. My mother would drop my sister and me off at the movie theatre and pick us up when the movie was over. So a *date* was going to the movie with a boy. It's funny how some things stand out in our memories. My first date was on September 4th; my first kiss from a boy (John) was on November 23rd. One weekend, my girlfriend, Kristie had a movie night at her house, and my boyfriend was there. After the movie, he kissed me by the pool table in her basement, and then he left. I later broke up with him on Valentine's Day because he tried to go all the way with me, and I wasn't ready.

On that same evening of my first kiss, Kristie and I were chatting about school, boys, parents, and general teenage issues. I had asked her if her father ever touched her. She gave me this look I'll never forget—she was absolutely horrified. Her response was, "Never." Then she asked me if my father ever touched me. My response was, "Almost every day." I didn't give her any graphic details because it was so embarrassing, but I did tell her he grabbed me, touched me in private areas, and kissed me on the lips all the time like adults do. She felt sorry for me, and we wept together. I made her promise not to tell her parents because I thought I would be in big trouble. This was my last visit to her house and she was never allowed to stay at my house again.

In my thirties, I visited Kristie, and she asked me how things were with my parents. I replied, "The same old, same old." She asked me if I remembered when her father stopped driving our school bus part way through the school year. I said that I did remember, but I didn't know why he had changed routes. It turns out Kristie had told her parents about the abuse, and her father was outraged. He refused to drive our school bus route anymore because he didn't know what he'd do if he ever saw my father while picking us up, or dropping us off. Again, we wept together. As a teenager, I didn't understand why I wasn't allowed to stay at her place, or why she couldn't come out to mine. As an adult, I fully understand.

I'm not sure exactly how old I was when my mother had surgery—it was sometime in my teens. It was a few days I'll never forget. My father had the opportunity he'd always wished for. He could play house with me while my mother was gone. I think my brothers were at my grandparents and my sister was at home with us. It was pure hell for me. My father grabbed me whenever he wanted. At night, he slept in my bed naked, made me sleep naked, and touched me everywhere. In the morning, he showered with me. And during the day, he kissed me all the time. Every day I went to school crying. I hated it so much, but didn't know how to get away.

During that time, I remember running into the washroom at school because I couldn't stop the tears, and I was convulsing from crying so hard. A classmate stuck her head over the top of the stall, and asked me what was wrong. I screamed at her, "How would you like it if you had to sleep naked with your father every night?" She left and could never look me straight in the eye again. The teachers either ignored me, or didn't care to know why I was upset.

During those few days my mom was in the hospital, my father showed me where a boy's penis should go if they decided to "stick it in me." My father never penetrated me, but he put his penis where a boy's should go. Then he showed me what boys like, how to touch and stroke their penis, and how they like to be kissed and hugged. It was a few days I can still vividly remember today as I write about it.

Once my mother returned home, I begged her to never leave me alone with my father ever again. Nothing changed.

DOUGLAS

I was 15 years old when I met Douglas. He was the man of my dreams. I saw him as the perfect guy, and the perfect way for me to escape the abuse I was receiving at home. He asked me out and I accepted. Two months later, my mother took me in to see the doctor to put me on birth control pills. Too late: I was already pregnant.

I knew a little bit about sex, from what my father taught me, but he didn't teach things about how women worked, or about getting pregnant. My mother threw a book on my bed when I started my period. I can't remember the name of it, but it was pink and told how girls bleed every month, and that's all I knew.

My parents discussed abortion and adoption with me, and I said no way. I saw my pregnancy as my chance to get away for good. I had tried to run away a month before, but was caught at Douglas' parents' house. My parents came over and said I lied about being abused, and not to believe anything I said. Douglas had already told his parents about the abuse because he had witnessed it himself a couple of times when he'd come to pick me up on dates. I wouldn't be in the house, so he'd drive around the farm looking for me, and then he'd catch my father in the act. Douglas and my dad actually had a couple of shoving matches, and some name calling incidents following Douglas finding us. My parents told Douglas' parents he was a drug user. They blamed him for planting ideas about abuse in my mind. In the end, my father told Douglas never to set foot on his land again. The next morning I went back home.

The only change was that I wasn't allowed to see Douglas anymore because he was a bad influence on me. I still worked very hard on the farm, continued going to school, and was abused throughout my entire pregnancy. I would lay in bed eating soda crackers every morning, hoping they'd stay in my stomach, so I could go to school. If I was lucky, I would make it through the day without becoming ill. I would come home from school, change my clothes, and do chores.

Just as I was approaching the corrals, it would hit me. The smell would fill my nostrils. I'd choke back the vomit as long as I could then the morning sickness would become afternoon sickness until I was finished doing chores. I don't remember one time during my pregnancy when I didn't become ill while doing my chores.

My parents knew I was ill. They saw me from the house stopping in my tracks, leaning over, and throwing up. If I was lucky, I'd make it to the fence, so I had something to prop me up. I ended up in the hospital on an IV for a week because the vomiting wouldn't stop, and Gravol just wasn't working anymore. My parents treated me the same as any other day—I got no special breaks for being pregnant.

My mother knew what it was like to be pregnant, she had four children. I wonder why a mother would allow her child to endure such intense pain. After all, being pregnant should be a beautiful experience. In the back of my mind, I thought they wanted me to miscarry, but that I would not allow.

The summer progressed and my belly grew. I started lactating, so I had to wear nursing pads to keep from staining my shirt. My father decided he would show me how to express the milk from my breast, so I wouldn't have to wear the pads. I still can visualize that exact moment. He hugged me and held me down, opened up my shirt, undid my bra, and started sucking on my nipples a little bit, and then he squeezed them, so the milk came out. I cried and cried and cried. I begged him to stop. I tried fighting back by kneeing him, but that infuriated him and made it worse. I felt like I was in hell with no way out. My mother had gone to town at the time and wasn't around, as usual. I couldn't tell her anyway. If I had, my father would have created more abuse just like he had in the past. And expressing milk with him was so embarrassing. Yuck!

WINNIPEG

A month later an opportunity presented itself for my sister and me to visit relatives in Winnipeg. We jumped on it. I phoned Douglas, told him when and where we'd be, then we headed for the big city. I started working up the courage to talk to my uncle and cousin about the abuse, but I couldn't do it. I was so embarrassed, and I remembered what had happened the other times when I did tell someone. Nothing changes, I thought, and telling someone just makes it worse for me at home. I met Douglas for coffee and we discussed my options.

We went to The Children's Aid Society (now called Child and Family Services). I reported everything that happened to me as far back as I could remember. They told me they were sorry, but I was out of their jurisdiction, and they couldn't help me. We couldn't believe it. It was a nightmare that seemed never ending. So, I went back to my relatives' house. My uncle sat me down, and asked me what was going on. For a minute there, I thought maybe he was asking about the abuse, but what he really was asking was if my parents knew Douglas was here? I was totally and completely exhausted. I'd had lost all hope of ever getting away. I said no, they didn't know he was with me, and nothing was going on anyway.

Who was going to help me? The people I thought could help me wouldn't. I was screwed no matter how I looked at it. My uncle informed my parents of Douglas' presence in the city and for some reason, it was decided my sister and I would get a ride back home with Douglas instead of taking the bus.

Maybe there is a God after all. We left first thing in the morning and headed home. Two-thirds of the way home is a smaller city, Brandon, with a Child and Family Services office, which happened to have jurisdiction over me. We went straight to that office, and I reported the same things I'd said in Winnipeg. My sister and I went to a foster home that night. She was so upset with me. I told her I couldn't take it anymore. She didn't know what it was like because Dad had never touched her.

My parents arrived the following day. They said I had cooked up this story because I was pregnant, and wanted to be with Douglas. They told CFS to call the RCMP in our small town and they would verify that Douglas was a trouble maker and drug user. That afternoon, we drove home with our parents. I was totally crushed. I had taken the biggest step in my life. It felt like a huge leap and, yet no one believed me. All I could think about was, "Boy, am I going to be in trouble when I get home."

OUR NEW HOME

When we arrived home my parents sat me down. They said they couldn't believe the lies I had told just because I wanted to live with Douglas. I said they weren't lies and they knew it. I was so angry. They knew I was telling the truth. What a big cover up. How could they sit there and deny everything that had happened? I thought I must be going insane.

They decided I should move out and go live with Douglas because I was going to do whatever it took, including ruining their reputation, to be with him. So, I did, a month later—a month before my daughter was born. Douglas and I rented my grandparents' old house in a town 10 miles away. I was supposed to start Grade 10 in September, but the morning sickness lasted all day and we had harvesting to do. The day after Douglas and I moved in together, the morning sickness was gone. I didn't get morning sickness again until the next time I became pregnant. I was so happy, ecstatic actually! My baby was almost here; I was living with my boyfriend, and getting ready to be a mother. The nursery was set up, and the countdown was on until delivery day.

I was getting ready for bed, around 11 p.m. on October 24, 1983. I felt really unsettled. I couldn't stand, couldn't sit. Maybe a bath would be good for me, I thought. I was just about to lift my foot and get into the tub, and whoosh! My water broke.

It was a girl! Tasha was born at 9:25 a.m. on the 25th of October. Now, I was a mother. I was so scared. What if I dropped her? How would I know if she was hungry, or needed her diapers changed? Would I wake up at night if she cried? We weren't prepared to be parents at the ages of 16 and 18. I didn't know how to cook, clean, or do laundry. I had always worked outside the house. I burned everything I cooked and used to boil over the soup at my mother's house because I always used the high setting on the element.

One night, I decided to make popcorn—using the high setting, of course. We didn't have a microwave, so I had to make popcorn the old fashioned way. I left the oil on high for about 10 minutes then decided it should be warm enough to throw the popcorn in. Poof, flames jumped out of the pot, the smoke alarm was going off, and I was yelling. Douglas came running into the kitchen, put the lid back on the pot and told me, "Get the fuck out of the kitchen. You're never fucking cooking again." Poor

Douglas must have thought what the hell did I get myself into? She can't even cook!

Douglas elicited the help of his parents, and I learned how to cook, do laundry, and be a good wife and mother.

My parents visited occasionally, but the animosity between my father and Douglas was too much for them to handle. So my father started visiting when Douglas was at work. This situation was not good. My father would watch me breast feed my daughter, and would take the blanket off I had covering her and myself. The feelings of freedom I had experienced before Tasha's birth were gone, ripped away by my father once again invading my life. After everything that had happened, why the hell would my mother let him come over by himself? What the hell was wrong with her?

Not long after that, I went back to school. I wasn't producing enough milk for Tasha and she was starving. So we switched her over to Enfalac baby's formula, which made it easier for me to attend school. We made arrangements with Douglas' parents to babysit during school hours. I picked up one course before Christmas, then four courses in the New Year.

STRUGGLING WITH EMOTIONS

I was still struggling with emotions if Douglas touched me in a way my father had. If I was touched in a certain way, my skin would crawl. I would fill with negative emotions related to my childhood abuse and be completely turned off. It wasn't his fault and I tried explaining to him how I felt, but he didn't understand. He was 18 years old and hadn't been exposed to sexual abuse.

A month after our daughter was born, Douglas decided he wanted sex . He wasn't taking no for an answer. I kicked, punched, and hit him, but it didn't matter. When he was finished, I told him he'd raped me, whether he saw it that way, or not. I told him I was still tender from giving birth and was not ready for sex, nor did we have protection, and I wasn't ready for another child at the age of 16. Douglas felt so bad that he tried to commit suicide. He had a gun aimed at his head and he pulled the trigger. Thank God he missed. He left the bullet in the wall to remind himself he never wanted to go there again.

We survived Christmas. In the New Year however, we started having problems with the wiring in my grandparents' house, so my grandmother asked my father to fix it. During one of my father's visits, a friend of Douglas' stopped by. He was asking me questions about Douglas, trying to find out if he had any pot. I was standing at the door mimicking the cut-throat sign as my father was in the basement working on the wiring. I didn't want him to hear, but the guy just didn't get it.

The next day my parents came to our house, packed up me, my daughter, and our belongings. They said because I wasn't eighteen, they had the right to make me move home. Their reason for the big move was that no daughter of theirs was going to be a drug addict. I couldn't believe it. I was finally happy living my life, and it was turned upside down, yet again.

Since moving in with Douglas, I had learned a lot about illegal drugs, different names for them, how they worked, and how easily available they were. I'll admit I tried most of them, and most of them I didn't like. We never did them around Tasha. She would be at his parents or with a babysitter at home and we would be elsewhere. I made it very clear to Douglas that my children would not be exposed to drugs by us. He always said, "My kids will smoke their first joint with me. I know how it works and they'll be safe trying it with me." So, I felt I had only two options. Stay at my parents' house, and be abused by my father, or live with a boyfriend, who was heavily into the drug scene.

The Monday after my parents took me to their house, I was off to school, and my mother was babysitting Tasha. I got off the bus, went to my first class, and then decided to go to the RCMP across the road. I gave a full statement of everything including the abuse, going to Children's Aid, moving out, and being forced to move back. That weekend, I was back living with Douglas again. It was made very clear I was not welcome in my parents' home.

A week later, my father showed up at my school, he wanted me to go for a ride in the truck with him and I said no, I didn't think that was a good idea. He asked me to at least come out to the truck and talk to him, so I did. After several minutes of chatting, he convinced me to get in the truck to talk to him.

We drove around for a while before he headed to the RCMP station. He wanted me to say I lied about everything. He wanted me to change my statement. We went in to the office and talked to a constable who just happened to play hockey with my father. The three of us sat in the room and they tried to get me to change my statement. I refused. I looked at my father and said, "You need help. What you are doing is wrong. Can't you understand that?" My father said I was lying. He said I made the whole thing up to be with Douglas. He left the room and I told the constable, "He needs counseling. And I'm not changing anything." He asked me about pressing charges and I said, "I don't want my father to go to jail; I just want him to have counseling." The constable then told me how bad a person Douglas was and how he was always in trouble with the RCMP. I walked out the door and walked back to school.

THE MARRIAGE

When I finished school, we moved to Melita, about 45 minutes south of the small town we had been living in. Douglas had a job in the oil industry and had been doing the long drive to work every day. We found a nice house, his parents bought it for us, and we were to pay them rent until it was paid in full. Then it was to be ours.

Life was okay. We fought like a married couple and made up the same way. I was seeing less and less of Douglas because of the long hours he worked. Eventually I found out he was a lot heavier into the drugs than I had believed. The long hours he was "working" included partying afterwards.

We became engaged, and were planning a wedding for August 1985. Because I was now 18, I didn't need my parents' permission to get married. Two weeks before the wedding, I was ready to leave Douglas. I was so scared. Where was I going to go? What should I do? Who would I call? I didn't know anyone except his parents, and they wouldn't help me. He was their son, after all. The only people I had to help me were my parents, and I only spoke with them about the wedding day and arrangements prior to the wedding. I tried phoning them and phoning them for two days. No answer. So, I stayed. I confronted my fiancé about the drugs and partying. He promised no more drugs, said things would change, that he loved me so much, and didn't want to lose me. A few days later he attempted suicide, a second time, by crashing his car into a bridge railing. Later, he said he couldn't live without me, and that he would change.

In the end, however, we were married on August 10, 1985. Life was good for the next months. I found out I was pregnant with my second child. This time, I suffered only four months of morning sickness and then it was completely over. What a change from my first pregnancy.

The oil company closed shop, and Douglas got a job working for a farmer nearby. He was home every evening and most weekends, and our life was still pretty good. On August 14th, our son, Terry was born. The next few months were rough. Douglas lost his job, bills weren't being paid, and utilities were cut off as a result. We decided to move to Alberta because the oilfield was booming and he had experience in the oil patch.

The first two months in Alberta were awesome. We were in love, raising our children, living the dream, and it was great. Then he met some guys at work who were into the drug scene. All hell broke loose. I got a job to help support the family. The kids hated it, they were used to having mom around 24/7, and now I was gone. Then spring came. Road bans were on and the oil patch basically shuts down until the bans are off. We moved back to our home in Melita. It was nice being home again, but home meant the old friend and in-laws were waiting, along with all the expectations and baggage they came with. Douglas' parents continued to help us financially as well as with repairs around the house.

I remember one winter evening Douglas' father left our home after a day of working on the house. Shortly after, Douglas' buddy came over, and they were smoking up. My father-in-law returned as he had been in an accident, and had walked back to our house. He never said anything until the next day. Then he asked me if Douglas was doing drugs and I said, "No."

Douglas' father was a beautiful man with a heart of gold. He respected me, helped us with the house, and loved his grandchildren dearly, so lying to him was extremely difficult for me. Douglas always said, "If my parents ask about the drugs, the answer is no. If they find out, we'll lose our house, and they won't help us anymore." So, as hard as it was, I lied.

Now my mother-in-law was a real piece of work—very controlling. She looked after us by buying clothes and food, but we never talked to her, or told her anything of much importance as she would hold the information over us as a form of control. She bought our clothes, she bought our food. It wasn't, "Let's go on a shopping trip." It was, "Here, I bought these for you." Don't misunderstand me; we appreciated everything his parents did for us. The issue was them not asking us what we thought, or asking for our opinion before his mom purchased things for us. A few months after being questioned by Douglas' father, I would find out exactly how controlling she really was.

Douglas and I had been arguing more and more about simple things. I wasn't allowed to go anywhere unless he or his parents were with me. We had three vehicles, but I wasn't allowed to drive by myself, and he made sure I didn't by taking all the keys when he left. I didn't have any friends, and felt very secluded from the rest of the world. It was the children and I at home every day, day after day after day. I love my children very much, but all parents need a break sometimes, and need to be with other adults. *Stir crazy* I believe is the phrase used to describe the situation.

I convinced Douglas to let me open a restaurant to help support us because our finances were terrible. The children would be with me at work, so I wouldn't have to pay a sitter, and at that point any money coming in would help. He was working in the same yard, so he could keep an eye on me. I would keep the children with me during the day, and another lady would work at the restaurant on the weekends. Douglas' parents also helped look after the children, and bought us groceries and necessities to keep us going. The money finally started coming in and it looked like we were finally going to get out of debt, but that's when he started partying more. That meant money was tight again. It was a vicious cycle that kept going around and around, never ending.

I tried leaving a few times, but he would stop me by standing in front of the door, or pulling me away from the door, so I couldn't leave. Once I tried crawling out the living room window. I made it half way and he dragged me back in again. I felt like a prisoner in my own home. We didn't have money to survive, yet he had money to buy drugs. He always said, "We'll double our money, trust me." Then we'd empty the children's bank accounts just so we could survive.

In July, I called my parents and told them I needed help. They were the only people who I knew who could help me, and who believed me about the drugs. Douglas had kept me secluded living in the country. I was isolated. I had no friends, no one I could talk to other than his parents, and I couldn't even tell them everything that was going on. I didn't realize it at the time, but Douglas was controlling me just as much as his mother was controlling us. When Douglas and I first moved in together, I had taken photos of him smoking up with a mask on. My parents had gone through my belongings after one of the times I moved back home. They kept these photos and negatives in case I needed them for legal purposes. Or so they said.

The weekend I left the children were at Douglas' parents. I didn't realize at the time that that would cause a great deal of issues for me. He decided he wasn't going to let them live with me or even see me for that matter. So the children stayed at his parents' house.

Douglas and I tried mediation, but it didn't work. We couldn't even talk with each other without one of us hanging up. And if I thought I was controlled by him and his mother before, it only became worse. When I was finally allowed to see the children, I would sit with them in the entry way of his parents' home with his mother standing watch over me. I would play with them for an hour then leave.

When I met Douglas and the children at the park, I had to give him my keys, so I wouldn't "kidnap" the children. Most of the arguing and fighting during that period was due to Douglas' mother's interference. She thought I would take advantage of Douglas. She was sure I would clean him out. And she thought I was a terrible mother, which she made very clear in front of my children, Douglas, and her husband, whenever she had the chance.

It's pretty hard to clean somebody out and take advantage of them when they don't have anything except a pile of debt. Douglas' financial state worked to his advantage when it would come time to paying child support. Unfortunately, the judge bought into his poor-me story.

In September of 1987, we agreed to joint custody with me having primary care. Douglas finally realized he wouldn't be able to look after the children by himself, didn't want to burden his parents with raising his children, and knew that I wanted the children with me.

BRANDON

The children and I moved to Brandon. I had a student loan, and was taking a cosmetology course. My childhood girlfriend Kristie was also in Brandon, and we became roommates.

One weekend we went to my parents, left the children with my mom, and headed into the local hotel for some girl time. We were drinking socially, but then came the shooters. Douglas walked into the bar, so we drank some more. He asked me to go outside with him and talk and I did. He wondered how the children and I were and if I was okay because I looked pretty drunk. At that moment, I started throwing up. Too many shooters will do that to a person. Somehow the conversation moved to overdosing on aspirin. I told him I had taken two aspirin early that evening because I had a headache. He thought I overdosed and took me to the hospital. There weren't any doctors available, so they sent me in an ambulance to Melita because they, too, thought I had overdosed. They wouldn't listen to me because I was drunk. They didn't end up pumping my stomach because I was throwing up already.

I stayed overnight for observations, then went home the next day. My mother was furious. "How dare you try to commit suicide especially while being at home? What do you want? Are you just looking for attention?"

I explained to my mother this was completely blown out of proportion; it was the shooters that made me ill and I was not trying to kill myself! What an experience. Never at anytime did my mother tell me I should get help, that maybe I should talk to a counselor. Kristie and I packed up the children and headed back to Brandon.

Kristie and I had a pretty sweet arrangement. She would watch the children for me, and in return, I didn't charge her any rent. It was a great arrangement until I started going to the bar more often. A group of girls from school would go out every Thursday night, and they invited me to go along with them. It felt so great to get out, so I started doing it more and more. I still went to school, paid my bills, and spent time with the children, just not as much as I should have. Needless to say my arrangement with Kristie didn't last very long. I couldn't afford both the apartment and paying for childcare, so I moved to a cheaper two bedroom trailer. There, a lady would come in and look after the children while I went to school. It was also an awesome arrangement until one day I decided to go for supper and to the bar after school without telling her.

Needless to say, I was on the hunt for another babysitter. I found one in the trailer court where we lived, but she already had lots of children, and said it was only temporary until I found another, which I took care of a couple of weeks later.

VANCE

One night on our girl's night out, I met a nice man at the bar and we became great friends. He was into weight lifting and introduced me to a healthy lifestyle. Because his gym was set up in his basement, I could work out and have the children with me. They would bring toys and play in the corner.

During a workout session in November, I met one of his roommates, Vance. Vance asked me out and we started dating. He was another drug user; how come I didn't see that one coming? Obviously I hadn't learned my lesson yet, and needed to go through more garbage. At this point, I started giving up on life. I started missing school, and fell into a deep depression. I kept going around in a circle, and thought this was just how my life was always going to be.

My father had come into Brandon, and was supposed to be staying at my aunt and uncle's. He showed up on my doorstep one night at 2 a.m. He said he couldn't sleep because of the furnace cutting in all the time. I was scared and called a couple of friends to come over to protect me. This was after I made a bed up for him on the couch, and told him to stay there. But at 2 in the morning, no friends were willing to come over, and Vance wasn't answering his phone. Half an hour later, my father was in my bed touching me. I fought him off for two hours, finally he went back to the couch, and I cried myself to sleep.

Now, with Vance in my life, I figured, what the hell? I was destined to a life of abuse and drugs, so why not just accept it? I started smoking pot three times a week after school and before I picked up the children. I also smoked on weekends when they were at their grandparents' house. Some of the drugs I had done with Douglas I was doing again, and I was drinking quite a bit. I called it partying and living my life the way I wanted to. The more I smoked up and drank, the less I remembered about the abuse.

Then, without warning, I got very ill. Oh, no! I thought; I couldn't be! But, oh, yes. Hello! Wake up call! I was pregnant again. And just a few weeks earlier, I had found Vance in bed with another woman and I ended our relationship on the spot. We had left school early that day and he wasn't expecting me. My workout friend had tried to drop hints that Vance was seeing someone else, insisting I could do better than Vance, and questioning how could I be sure Vance was being faithful to me? He wasn't. And there I was, pregnant and on my own again.

That weekend I went home to my parents, and had a really good chat with my sister about our childhood. I asked her if our father had ever touched her and if it had affected her life. She said our father had tried to touch her once after I'd left. She told him if he ever tried it again, she would do the same thing I did and report him. My sister said he never tried touching her again. So, I had protected her. At least something good came out of all those years of abuse.

I was feeling pretty great following that conversation. So great, that I decided to attend a social with a group of friends. There I met Charles. Too bad that I had just found out I was pregnant. Here I was trying to move forward with someone else and now I was being pulled back, yet again.

I got tired of my landlord at the trailer park not fixing things that were broken. Especially after someone had broken the locks and got into the trailer while I was away one weekend. Even then, he wouldn't fix the broken locks. I felt very unsafe and paranoid that someone would break in again. I reported the incident to the police. They dusted the trailer for finger prints, but nothing came of it. For my own piece of mind, I moved out and into a new place closer to school.

Now I was pregnant, living in a one bedroom suite with two kids on the top floor of a house. Terry slept in the playpen in my room, and Tasha slept on the couch. I talked to my mom and Charles about the pregnancy, and we decided the best thing to do would be to end the pregnancy. I knew the drugs and alcohol hurt the baby because of the excessive amount I had been doing. I'd seen babies with Fetal Alcohol Syndrome, sometimes hooked up to machines and deformed. I just couldn't bring a child like that into the world. I was a single mother, going to school, living in a shack, and I was going to bring another child into this mess? After many long discussions, I had an abortion. I quit drinking, but still smoked pot every once in a while. Soon the guilt set in about the abortion, and what I'd done to another living being. Had I known what I know now, I would recognize that I was suffering from depression. But I didn't know what was wrong, so I just kept going, struggling everyday to stay sane.

I finished cosmetology school in May of 1988, packed up the children, and went to work in a shop in small town Manitoba. Far away from everyone except my children and Charles.

CHARLES

Charles and I became very close, very fast, and a few months later we moved in together. I commuted to Grandview until the owner found a replacement for me. Afterwards, I opened up my own shop in the house we moved into in small town Saskatchewan. Finally, I knew where I belonged. Charles and I joined mixed curling, spent time camping, and life was very good. There was a bit of tension between Charles and the children, but I thought with time they'd become closer.

Then, one day I noticed how many empty beer bottle cases we had stacked in the basement. I had quit drinking, so none of those bottles were mine. Then I realized that whenever we visited friends or family, I always drove home because Charles was too drunk to drive. His drinking was getting worse. The children would hate it when I went for walks, but I never really understood why. Years later, Tasha told me that every time I left, Charles would send her and Terry to their rooms, and tell them to stay there until I got home. They weren't his children, so he felt he didn't have to look after them.

Once we got engaged, I got caught up in how beautiful my engagement ring was, as well as in the whole process of planning a wedding for the following summer. Eventually, I was having serious second thoughts about getting married though. I headed to Brandon to visit Kristie, and try to sort things out. We first went to a bar, then to a party. That's where I met a really attractive man. One thing led to another, and I headed home the next morning with the knowledge I wasn't ready to get married.

I told Charles about sleeping with another man, that I wasn't ready to marry him—that we had a lot of things to work through. I gave him back the ring, and said I should move out. In the end, he gave *me* back the ring, and we stayed together for a few more months.

I couldn't handle life anymore. I couldn't sleep at night—the guilt of cheating on Charles was eating me up. Yet, I knew he wasn't the person I was going to spend the rest of my life with anyway. I think he knew, too, because he was drinking more than usual.

I got a job in a convenience store in Moosomin. I thought if I started getting out maybe I'd make some new friends, and would get more confidence. I still had the hairdressing business on the side and worked a few days a week doing that.

On my evening shifts at the convenience store, a man named Patrick would always come in, and buy an apple to take to work the next day. He said it got him out of the house, and it was nice walking in the evenings. We became friends and started chatting more and more on those evening shifts.

Charles and I were growing apart, and my cheating on him was the cause of it. It was my fault that the relationship was where it was. I also knew I didn't want to marry him. So I decided to move out. Patrick offered to help and had found a couple of rental houses for me to look at, so off I went.

It just so happened that Charles showed up while I was gone from the store. He was waiting for me when I returned. He, of course, assumed I was cheating on him again, which I honestly wasn't. Then the arguing began. Our relationship was now officially over.

MY BROTHERS

Instead of moving into the house I had looked at with Patrick, I moved back to my parents. I'm not really sure why. Maybe to prove to Charles I wasn't cheating on him, or because I was scared to be on my own raising two children. I enrolled in school to work on getting my Grade 12. Because I was over 19, I qualified for the adult diploma program. Mom watched the children while I went to school.

One night, I woke up and my brother had his hand over me, and was playing with my nipple. I pushed him off, and told him to go to his own room. I was dazed and confused for a while trying to figure things out. Then I remembered touching him one night when I was 12 or 13 years old. I had been babysitting my siblings, and for whatever reason, I wanted to see what his penis looked like and if it did the same things my father's did when I milked the cow. I know he told my parents about it because my father confronted me a few days later, and I had to show him exactly what I had done to my brother. I thought what goes around comes around. I touched him when he was younger and now he was touching me.

I discussed the situation with my mother and she said, "If you can't get along with your brother, then maybe you better move out." In other words, she didn't believe me.

That's when the children and I moved into town. I rented a house, found a sitter, and kept going to school. My father came into town to fix a few things in the house. I was now 21 years old. If you think the abuse would be a thing of the past, you would be wrong. My father was working on a tap in the washroom, and I was helping him. He grabbed me, and pulled me on his knee; he started fondling my breasts. I was shocked: I couldn't believe what was happening. I asked him to leave and he did. I phoned Charles crying and crying about what had just happened. He drove out that night and stayed with me. At 1:00 a.m., I phoned my parents' home. I talked to my mother and told her my father was not allowed to see me by himself ever again. I was sick and tired of him touching me and it was going to stop now. Then I asked to speak with my father. I told him he was not allowed to touch me again. If he did, I would go straight to the police, and have him charged.

At this point, Charles and I were actually trying to work things out. We had been talking ever since I had moved back to my parents' home. My two concerns were his drinking, and his not wanting the children around. Whenever we did something together, I had to find a babysitter because when he came over, he wanted the children gone. He always said it was because he didn't want them to hear us, but I didn't believe him.

In April, we headed to my parents' house for a birthday party. His parents and niece were invited and attended. Shortly after our arrival, Charles' niece came in crying and upset, saying she wanted to go home. She wouldn't explain her reason for wanting to leave. So, our visit was cut short; I soon found out why.

Constable Bobby phoned me about a week later and asked me to come down to the RCMP office. She needed to talk to me about something. I had no idea what was going on, and was not prepared for what happened next.

The school runs a program about telling secrets. The teachers read a book about a little boy who has secrets. The book tells how it's safe to tell secrets to another adult. Then the teachers ask the students if they have any secrets. My daughter stood up and said she had a secret. She said her uncle's touched her all the time in her private places, and threatened if she ever told on them, they would beat her up.

When the constable told me this I was horrified. I had always protected my children from my father; I made sure they were never alone with him. Never in my wildest dreams did I ever think of my brothers touching them. So, I gave a statement about the past, the birthday party, and what opportunities I knew of that my brothers had for this to happen. I was absolutely mortified. How could I have not protected my children? How could my brothers have done such a thing to my children, to hurt my children—and possibly other children—like that? I was completely horrified.

Then the anger set in. Who the hell did they think they were dealing with? One pervert in our family was enough, now we had two more. That was unacceptable as far as I was concerned. Nobody could stop my father, but these two teenage brats were going to be stopped immediately.

A few days later, Constable Bobby called and asked me to come in again. She had talked to Charles' parents and found out my brother had the two girls in the truck and wouldn't let them out until they lifted up their skirts, took off their panties, and let him touch them. Charles' niece got out of the truck before anything happened and headed straight for her grandparents. When the commotion had started, we went looking for the children. Luckily, my daughter had been saved from abuse that one time.

Constable Bobby came to the house in street clothes to talk to the children. She needed statements from the children on the allegations. I spoke with Douglas' mother, my ex-mother-in-law, and she told me the children were both playing a lot with their private parts and it had only started recently. Eventually, we found out they had both been touched on several occasions. Next, we took a trip to Brandon to the RCMP office. It was equipped with dolls and a comfortable living room setting to put the children at ease. They were asked to point to where they had been touched and show how they had been touched. The interviews were separate and each was videotaped. Because my brothers were minors, nothing much was required of them as a result of their actions other than counseling. Whether or not they ever went, I have no idea. I did, however, find out about counseling for myself. This was the first I had ever heard of getting help for me, and for my issues. This was a game changer.

So off I drove to Brandon once a week for five weeks. The set up was a group of women met with a counselor and we each told our stories. Some stories were worse than mine and some were not, but the important thing was that I realized that I was not alone. It was very difficult for me to talk about the abuse in front of other women. I know they were just as uncomfortable as I was because of the tears everyone shared in the group. When someone's kept a secret as long as we had, it was very difficult to unbury and reveal it, let alone discuss it in a group setting.

As a result of my counselling, I finally had an understanding of my mother's attitude toward the abuse. She knew it was happening, but for her own reasons chose not to leave my father. Whether she wasn't strong enough, or was too scared, I'll never know—she won't talk about it. No matter, I still wasn't ready to forgive her for her not doing something to stop it. Because she didn't act, my brothers eventually caught on and now, in turn, had abused my children. And that I could not forgive.

This whole episode, combined with the issue of my children being left out of our relationship so much, led me to finally break things off with Charles for good.

I graduated with my Grade 12 diploma in June of 1990, and headed down east to visit my aunt and uncle for a well deserved holiday.

PATRICK

Remember Patrick from the last chapter. I met up with him down east. We spent some time together, talked about life, where we wanted to go, and what we wanted to do. Since we seemed to have so much in common, and since I liked it there, I decided to rent an apartment and establish myself first, then send for the kids. I had applied for some jobs, and was waiting for the results. My aunt and uncle lived a couple of hours away, so I had family close by. Then Douglas caught wind of our moving plans, and had a court order issued saying the children could not leave the province without his consent. He refused to let them go, so back I went to Manitoba.

I ended up renting one of the houses I had previously looked at in Moosomin and started my hairdressing business again. Patrick and I had started dating at that point, and a month later, he moved back to Manitoba, and in with the children and me. A year later, we were married, and nine months after that, our daughter Anna was born. The ultrasound attendant told us we were having a boy, so we bought everything for our new baby in blue. Poor thing, in her first photos, she was covered all in blue. Maybe that's why she's a tomboy today. The pregnancy was easy. This time I had only two months of morning sickness. The hardest part for me was quitting smoking. I managed to quit in the second month and lasted until two weeks after she was born before I started again.

My new husband had a job opportunity he couldn't refuse, so we headed to Alida, Saskatchewan for a new start. His mother, who also lived in Moosomin, was very controlling, and always had something to say about how we were raising the children. Needless to say, moving away again seemed like a good thing for us.

We moved, set up house, and I worked part-time waitressing in the local hotel bar, and part-time hairdressing at home. Patrick worked for an oilfield construction company driving truck. Our lives were pretty good. We did fight occasionally, but for the most part, our relationship was solid. Then road bans came on in the spring and he found himself without work. Needing an income, he went to work for my parents, which was probably the biggest mistake we ever made.

I remember it was Easter, we went to a social in town, and I saw classmates I hadn't seen for years. I introduced them to Patrick, said how happy I was, that we had a daughter, etc. He knew another fellow who helped my father, so he sat with him and chatted. We danced occasionally throughout the night. I thought we were both having a good time.

Near the end of the social, Patrick kept asking me, "What have you got against me?" I kept answering him, "Nothing, I love you. I've introduced you to my old friends, bragged about how happy we are. I have absolutely nothing against you." We ended up back at my parents' house. As I was putting out Easter candies, he flipped out on me, demanding again to know what I had against him. The dish went flying, candies went flying, and I was pressed up against a closet with his fist coming towards me. My mother walked down the stairs at that moment and told him to relax and go to bed. Later, I suggested we go to marriage counseling. He refused, so I went on my own.

Before I found a marriage counselor, I went to a psychiatrist. He had me fill out a 20-page questionnaire. The information was entered into a computer program. I was assessed based on the program's criteria. The psychiatrist told me I wasn't crazy, but the thought it would help to seek marriage counseling through the local mental health worker.

That's when I began realizing and acknowledging my insecurities, my lack of self-esteem, and how I had no confidence in myself as a mother or a wife. Once I realized and accepted these qualities, I began to grow and strengthen who I was. But as I presented my new found strength at home, the arguing between Patrick and me became worse, so—unfortunately—I quit seeing the counselor. Then when we argued, he'd grab my wrists, I'd get scared he was going to hit me, and I'd shut my mouth.

On the day of our last argument, Patrick hit the door behind me with his fist. That was the moment our marriage ended. The landlady never did like me, so she evicted me.

To get by, I was working part-time in a grocery store and part-time waitressing. Soon, I started seeing one of the regulars at the grocery store, which cost me my job. Oh, the scandal. Rumors were flying. The small town gossips had blown the conflict between Patrick and the new man out of proportion. First there was a scuffle. Afterwards, there were some punctured tires. In short, another big mess.

THE BREAKING POINT

Next, I moved to a small town of approximately 100 people. I got set up—rented a home, hairdressed a little, and to support myself, lived on welfare. I felt like such a failure. My second marriage ended. I was a single mom raising three children in a dead end town. To make matters worse, someone reported me to welfare because I was hairdressing, so welfare cut me off and were investigating me. For awhile, I couldn't sleep, then when I could, I would sleep all day and night. I barely ate anything, and lost a lot of weight. What kind of life could I possibly give my children? I couldn't afford swimming lessons, or skating, or anything extracurricular. I couldn't even afford to buy them food and clothes.

It was a dark period for me. Just to show how my mind was working, I kept thinking about ending it all. A few miles from our small town was a gravel road. On the road was a bridge. If I drove too fast, lost control of the car, I would fly off the bridge into the rocks 50 feet below me. Surely I would die instantly. This way the children would get my life insurance and they could go live with relatives. I had a will stating where I wanted them to live and how the money should be divided.

I couldn't believe I was thinking this way, but I couldn't stop it and eventually, the depressive thoughts took their toll on me. I ended up having a breakdown—as in a nervous breakdown. I was in the hospital for two weeks, heavily medicated, and placed on suicide watch. I spoke with my doctor daily about what I should do. In the end, I decided the children were better off living somewhere else. They would always have me, no matter what. I'd be just a phone call away. But they needed more stability than what I could offer them. They also needed someone more financially secure than I was to provide for them.

Tasha and Terry moved in with Douglas' mother and Anna moved in with her aunt. I, stupidly, moved back to my parents' house. I'd decided I was going back to school to take Business Administration, straighten out my life and finances, set myself up, and stabilize my mind, emotions, and spirit. Then I'd be ready for the children to join me again. My parents warned me they knew students who'd taken the same business course and then couldn't find jobs afterwards. "Check the paper and see what types of jobs are out there," they kept saying. So I looked and found ads for Class 1 Drivers. There were columns and columns of ads looking for truck drivers. Well, I thought to myself, I had the farming background, so why not give it a try?

ON THE ROAD

From 1994-1997, I put in three years of long haul driving with too many driving partners to count. That was because the company dispatchers I drove for prided themselves in setting up couples. "I set these two up and they're married today." Or, "These two are engaged because I set them up," etc. Needless to say, almost every trip I took was a potential set-up with a single male partner.

Meanwhile, I didn't want to have anything to do with these guys, or any man for that matter. I wanted to be by myself—lost and hidden from the rest of the world. I knew I'd made the right decision giving up custody of my children, but it still hurt like hell. I didn't want to be around anyone, especially men. I missed my children so much. I would cry at night in the bunk after I talked to them. My cell phone bills were $300 a month because I talked to them so often.

Eventually, it got to the point where I'd get in the truck and say, "Here's the line, don't cross it. If you cross it, I may leave you somewhere." The men usually figured

I was going to be their bunk bunny, but I set them straight pretty quickly. The schedule was tight. Two weeks on the road, four days at home. I'd drive to my parents, get the children for the weekend and drive back to work. This arrangement worked fine until the children moved in with Douglas.

Douglas soon had custody of the children and was playing a control game. He was telling the children I wasn't paying child support; therefore they couldn't do extracurricular activities. I'd call; he'd refuse to let me talk with them. We'd make arrangements for me to pick them up; he would change his mind, and tell the children I didn't want them. It was a total nightmare.

I felt so alone and scared that I took a bottle of ephedrine and decided to end my life. Ephedrine is essentially caffeine. It speeds up your heart rate. If you take enough, it will cause a heart attack. Lucky for me, a friend found me crashed on the floor, dragged me into the bathroom, shoved my finger down my throat, and basically saved my life.

During this same period, my youngest brother was also suffering from depression, undiagnosed, of course, just as mine was. One day, I received a call informing me my brother was missing, and that nobody had seen him for two days. I went to my parents to join the search parties.

With the help of the RCMP and a search plane, my brother's body was found on the second day I was home.

He was found with a single gunshot wound to the head, and gun powder on his hand. We never came across a note, so we can only speculate as to why he committed suicide. Was it feelings of guilt from abusing my children? Was he abused? Ironically, he had just bought a house, and was going on his own to farm. Was he feeling pressure from finances, or from living right beside my parents? Nobody really knows. It was an extremely emotional time for our family, and we were actually close for a few months. I swore to myself I would never put my children through that—any thoughts of committing suicide were thereafter forever gone.

My brother's death had me thinking about my own near death experience. I decided to make some changes. No more long haul driving for me. I got a job working days, driving short hauls. If I thought this was going to be any easier, I was wrong. I was gone from six in the morning to midnight. At least it kept me close to home. Another good thing about it was I was in the best shape of my life. Throwing tarps, chains, bear traps, and cinching straps a few times a day kept me very active. Even so, I knew this wasn't the right life for me. I often found myself wishing I had taken the Business Administration course I'd originally planned on.

When I did finally meet up with a female trucking partner whom I got along with, worked well with, and who could actually drive, the company gave us some bullshit excuse about how they'd work our days off differently because we lived in distant cities thirteen hours apart. In other words, they weren't very accommodating. So I quit.

To be honest, one motivating factor to leave trucking was that Tasha was ready to move back in with me, so I needed a normal job. In April of 1997, I attended the Academy of Learning and graduated with an honors diploma in Accounting. Off to work I went, to a 9-5 office job. I had finally began the process I'd intended to start four years earlier.

JACK

I met Jack and we soon became very good friends. Throughout the following year, we started dating, and eventually moved in together. Since Tasha was now ready to move back in with me, I thought, great, we can be one big happy family. Not!

Jack and Tasha clashed. I quit smoking at the time because Jack wanted me to. But I started again four months later because I couldn't handle the stress. I remember crying at work one day telling my boss I didn't want to go home. Tasha was rebelling, Jack was being stubborn, and I was thinking I needed to go back on medication. I was missing the warning signs that were there with Jack. The arguing with his ex-wife, the yelling and screaming. I thought, well, I did the same with my ex, Douglas, so who am I to judge someone else for the same thing? I kept ignoring the other red flags. Then Jack's daughter moved in with us, and the stress level went even higher. Now we had two teenagers rebelling, trying to find their paths, and pushing the limits every chance they got.

One evening the phone rang, Jack ran inside the house, pushed Tasha out of the way, and said, "This is my fucking house and I'll answer the phone around here." I told Tasha to pack a bag, and we were out the door. Jack followed me outside, asked me where I was going, and raised his fist to hit me. I'm not sure why he didn't hit me, if it was because Tasha was watching him, or the look in my eyes that threatened, "Just try it."

This time I stuck to my guns, and actually did move out. This was when I started my spiritual journey. Out of the blue one evening, my cousin called me and said, "Lisa, I just talked to this fortune teller, and she was so accurate about my life. You have to call her. Here's her number." So I ended up calling Jeannine in Ottawa. She'd been reading tarot cards and working with energy for many years. That knowledge was all I needed to trust her as a spiritual advisor. After talking with her, I bought *The Celestine Prophecy*, and started a whole new chapter in my life.

MY HOUSE

As a way of starting over, I came up with this brilliant plan to build my own house. When you're a single woman living in a Mennonite community, however, you do no such thing. To say it was a struggle is an understatement—this in spite of my having a lot of loving friends helping me with the construction.

To save some money for the new house, Tasha and I moved out of our apartment into a friend's home. Unfortunately, these so-called friends weren't quite as they appeared. The wife was very controlling and jealous. She lied to her husband constantly and was using drugs, which he knew nothing about. He was the nicest man I had ever met. I couldn't understand what was wrong with this woman. Couldn't she see how good she had it? My God, the man was good looking, had a full-time job, gave her whatever she wanted, and was so in love with her. He would have walked on water if she'd asked him to. I didn't last in that home very long. Tasha stayed, however, and later told me some pretty crazy stories about parties at the house when the husband was at work.

I moved in with a girlfriend I'd met at the Academy of Learning. Even though I worked fulltime, I was focused on building my house. My first big obstacle was getting a building permit. The problem was I was a woman, and I wasn't a contractor by trade. To get around that, a male customer from work got the permit for me, so I could at least get started. On June 1, 1999, a friend cleared the land with a front-end loader and construction began. I hauled gravel for the house and driveway. A friend used a skid-steer bobcat to pack the gravel. The rest of the work I did with the assistance of wonderful friends and their husbands. With all of us on the job, concrete was poured, walls went up, windows went in, and shingles went on.

Another challenge I faced was when I was shingling on a 30-degree Celsius day. The sun was melting the tar, the tar was melting the shingles and sticking them together, then oops! There was the slip of a knife, and off to the hospital I went for stitches. Seven stitches, a few fainting spells later, and then back to the house I went to finish shingling. Or so I thought; luckily for me, my dear friends retired me for the rest of that day.

On that same evening, my boss had a company barbeque for all our branch employees. I'm not a fan of volleyball, but this being the only time of year that I ever played, I couldn't be a bystander. Once I realized we had just enough people for two teams, I really felt pressured to play. The net was set up, the ball was full of air, and everyone was on the court while I went searching for a work glove to protect my newly stitched thumb. I at least took the trouble to wrap an extra pad of toilet paper around my bandaged thumb before I stuck my hand in the glove. I went on to play volleyball for the next two hours. Stubborn? I would say so! Trust me, I paid for it the next day as I found myself in a great deal of pain when I was shingling again.

I hired a plumber, electrician, drywall hangers, and a drywall taper to do the things I couldn't. Next came the painting. "Use oil-based primer and paint, that's the best thing for new drywall." I followed that advice, but what a mess I had. I stank like gas from trying to clean the paint off, not to mention that I had to be extra careful whenever I lit a cigarette! Those were crazy times. My hair, face, arms, and hands stayed covered in paint and I had pictures taken to back it up.

I have to say, I loved it, however. Every single minute of working on the house was so empowering. I felt strong and self-confident as I stood on my own as a single mom building a house. What an achievement for me! It took many long days and hard work, but it was well worth it in the end.

I can't believe what an eye-opener that experience was. It's amazing how some men in business think women are stupid. Let me clarify this. I would call for estimates for something to do with the house. Then I would have one of the guys from work call for a similar estimate, and their quote was always lower. Why do you suppose that is?

After getting the run around on so many other quotes, I thought I was finally getting a break when it came to installing my kitchen cupboards. The costs to buy them were astronomical as it was, never mind the costs for installation. When a friend came along and offered to help me in exchange for food and cigarettes, it sounded like a great deal.

The friend in question was John—the guy from whom I received my first kiss when I was fourteen. He reappeared in my life after my parents gave him my phone number. That's when he offered to help with the kitchen cupboards and miscellaneous small finishing touches. John was a construction worker, and was working close by in Winnipeg. Everything seemed so easy with him. Only after I accepted his offer, did I discover I had a new battle on my hands.

I guess John figured there would be fringe benefits with the job he was performing. He found out very quickly, however, that this was not to be the case. I did buy groceries and cigarettes for John and his helper as promised. I also let them sleep in the living room. I paid for all the materials they needed to do the finishing touches, along with the kitchen cupboards themselves. In return, and without notice, they left half way through the job. They also slapped a lien against me for $4500. And I didn't hear from them again. So, I contacted my lawyer, asked friends who had witnessed the two workers' behavior for sworn affidavits, and asked Tasha to give me a play-by-play of events while I was at work.

As it turned out, they had asked my daughter for drugs, stole cigarettes and any money I had laying around, slept most of the day, and started working just before I arrived home from work. Tasha's affidavit was added to the lawyers file as well as a video showing the mess they left, the poor workmanship on the cupboards, and the stud finder test holes in the ceiling. Meaning, they used a 3-inch spike (nail) and hammer, tapped it into the newly painted drywall looking for the stud. This left small, but clearly visible round circles all over the ceiling and walls that needed to be fixed.

In spite of this new battle, I was determined to make progress. I kept working on the house. The RM Office that gave me such a hard time about the building permit had for some reason decided not to run the natural gas piping down the road to my land. This was simply unacceptable, as all my water heaters were installed and they were to be fueled by natural gas. I contacted the local natural gas company and spoke with their rep Larry about our initial meeting regarding the piping out to my land. Larry contacted the RM Office and informed them the piping would be going in as originally planned. The RM Office tried to charge me $1000 for running the piping. In the end, I paid the same $500 deposit as everyone else on the road. Finally, on August 13th—not quite two and a half months after construction began—I officially moved into my new home. The one I built myself (with a lot of help, of course).

There was still plenty of work to be done. For instance, the siding was still going on, but it looked pretty darn good considering the walls only went up on the first of July. When the building inspector for the mortgage company came out to inspect the premises, he found I didn't have eaves troughs on the house, and he found that one of the large, second-hand windows I had used had condensation in between the panes of glass. Based on these two findings, he refused to release the rest of the mortgage funds until I fixed them. Back to the phone, back to getting estimates, back to calculating the differences only to discover it was cheaper to pull out the window and replace it with a new one than it was to fix it. Out the old window came, in the new window went. Never mind that I had to reinstall the siding on the outside wall, replace the drywall, and repaint. At least that problem was corrected. Later, a company came out and installed the eaves troughs. At last, all was fixed and ready for the inspector to return.

The inspector was good for his word and, with problems fixed, released the funds. The bank suggested I leave them where they were because of the lien. My plumber, however, was not impressed with me at this point because his payment happened to be tied up in the funds being held. A month later, my lawyer contacted me. John was in psychiatric ward and his lawyer was dropping the case. Two thousand dollars in legal fees and a ticked-off plumber, for what? What in the world was the lesson here? Be wary of those who say they will help you for free; most of the time, there is a hidden agenda buried in their psyche.

Beyond these sometimes frustrating lessons, the building project gave me a sense of self for the first time in my life. I was challenged daily, I persevered, and I built my own house. Thank God for the friends I had, for all their help and support because my family sure as hell wasn't there to help me.

My parents never actually saw my house. They saw a photo album full of pictures and heard the story of how I built it, but they were too busy farming and going down south for the winter. My sister and her son came to visit for a weekend, but that's about it. At first, I was hurt over their lack of interest, but then I realized I didn't want them in my space anyway. I built the house without them, I did it on my own, and I succeeded. I couldn't help but wonder why I still was trying to prove myself to them?

MY SPIRITUAL JOURNEY

Even as the house was being finished, I continued on my new spiritual journey. I read *The Tenth Insight* (another book by the author of *The Celestine Prophecy)*, as well as *Living in the Light* and *Creative Visualization* (both by Shakti Gawain). I also started reading tarot cards. My life was changing and I felt like I was on cloud nine. I would sit in the sunroom for an hour every morning and sometimes in the evenings with my plants, watching the energy around them, and meditate.

I would pray to Grandmother Moon (the full moon) once a month and thank her for all the wonderful people in my life and for answering my prayers. Slowly, I started seeing the colors around Grandmother Moon and seeing images within her. Some of the images were light- or dark-haired men holding flowers, laughing, and walking. The most vivid image I remember is of a couple holding hands with the trees in the background, sand under their feet, and them smiling at each other. Now that was the kind of love I was looking for!

As I delved deeper into my spirituality, I became more aware of the energy surrounding all living things. More aware of the beauty our earth contains. My visions became clearer and my meditative states deeper. One afternoon, a deer was looking at me through my garden doors, and I felt like I had finally found true happiness. I felt I found where I belonged. My spiritual side was awakening more and more every day, and I felt very much at peace with myself.

One evening, during a conversation with Jeannine, the tarot card reader, I channeled. Channeling means the transmission of information or energy from a nonphysical source through humans. Channelers, or mediums, are sometimes in an apparent trance during the communication. Sources for the information include angels, discarnate former humans, extraterrestrials, and levels of consciousness. I was on the verge of falling asleep when strange words started coming out of my mouth. They made absolutely no sense to me, but they made complete sense to Jeannine.

I felt new doors were opening. I was so happy with my life and the direction I was headed in. I had good friends who would visit, have coffee and chit chat. A couple of days before Christmas, I flew out to Ottawa to meet Jeannine. Life was absolutely amazing.

She introduced me to her spiritual friends, her family invited me to Christmas dinner, and I felt very accepted just the way I was. Jeannine invited me into her home, showed me crystals, and encouraged me to continue on my path of newfound spirituality. I flew home with a new perspective on life, ready to take on the world, but it soon came crashing down.

Tasha hated living in the country and was rebelling with a vengeance. I had apparently destroyed her life by moving to the country, and she made sure I knew it. Every single day!

TASHA

"I hate living here! You've destroyed my life. I'm stuck out here in the middle of nowhere!" Tasha screamed at me.

These were words I heard almost every day. I was trying to raise a teenager; I was willing to make up for lost time. So I accepted a lot of the chaos. I knew she smoked pot and hell, who was I to judge? I had done the same. I wasn't aware of the heavier drugs she was using until I received a call late one night. It was the hospital letting me know my daughter had been admitted for drug abuse. "A bad trip on acid," is how the nurse described it. The hospital reported the incident to the mental health worker in the area. From there, a series of unforgettable events unfolded.

Our first and only counseling session with the mental health worker lasted about an hour. Most of it consisted of Tasha and me yelling at each other and the counselor attempting to mediate. Tasha stood up, looked at me with pure hatred in her eyes and said, "I'm smoking pot until I'm 80 and there's nothing you can do to stop me." Then she walked out the door. That was the end of the session. The mental health worker said she couldn't help us. So much for family counseling.

So I started counseling on my own. Tough Love is the practice I followed. Set boundaries and keep them no matter what. The no-matter-what could be very trying at times. The curfew I set was 11:00 p.m., and if Tasha wasn't home by then, the door was locked. A few times she pushed the limits and came home five or ten minutes afterwards. One evening she came home at 11:15 p.m. and the door was locked. She started screaming at me through the door to let her in. The next day I talked to her, and we came to an understanding. That lasted about a week, and then we started all over again. I wasn't willing to give up on my daughter. Some nights she would come home stoned, some days she would sleep all day recovering from the night before. I have to give her some credit though. She was still in school and passing her courses. This lifestyle went on for months.

Finally, I decided enough was enough. I sold the house I built, and bought a bungalow in Steinbach. One month later, Tasha moved in with her boyfriend. A few months after that, she was back with me telling me she wanted to go to school in Winnipeg and that she could live on independent living. Independent living means a child can be legally emancipated and basically receive welfare as long as they continue to go to school. It would mean I would have to sign over all parental rights to Child and Family Services. Since my own experience with Child and Family Services was life altering in such a negative way, I did not trust the organization one bit. To put them in charge of my daughter's welfare was not something I was willing to do. Tasha stayed with friends in Winnipeg for the summer and got work piercing in a tattoo parlor. She seemed happy enough, but I later found out she really wasn't. Crystal meth, crack cocaine, and ecstasy were her drugs of choice.

During this time, counseling sessions began with Child and Family Services. Eventually Tasha moved to Winnipeg, and I eventually signed over all parental rights to CFS after all. That was an extremely emotional situation for me as a parent watching my 16-year-old daughter walk out the door as an adult, while knowing she was a drug addicted teen. All I could do was be there for her when she needed me.

Little did I know that while all of this was happening with Tasha, more confusion was to be added to my life. I received a phone call from the local RCMP detachment and was asked if I could come down for questioning. I'm thinking to myself, what's Tasha done now?

"We'd like to discuss a relationship you had with a gentleman in 1997, Mr. Jack Dawson." I said, "Okay."

The constable said, "Mr. Dawson's daughter has filed a complaint against him for sexual abuse, and these are some of the non-sexual instances she felt you would be able to shed some light on." I was flabbergasted. Abused? When? Where was I? Oh my God, is this what my mother went through? No, it wasn't what my mother went through. The instances were about Jack physically pushing her around, and comments he had made. The alleged sexual abuse happened after Tasha and I moved out.

A few months later, I was called into a court room and asked to testify against Jack. I was really nervous and started crying when the prosecutor asked if I had written a book in 1997, and left it out where Jack's daughter could read it? Was it a book describing sexual abuse? I answered, "Yes." The judge asked me if I needed a few minutes and I shook my head no. The tears were pouring down my face, but the truth needed to be told. The prosecutor continued with his questions for another twenty minutes.

I left the court room shaking and crying. Thank God my girlfriend was with me and could drive me home. A few days later, Jack showed up at my work place. He said, "The judge based his decision mainly on your testimony, and I want you to change it. You know I would never do those things to my daughter. You lied in the court room because you're mad at me." I asked Jack to leave my office and he did. I never changed my testimony because I had told the truth.

I asked Tasha if she knew anything about sexual abuse with Jack's daughter, or if he had ever touched her. She said no on both counts. Tasha and Jack's daughter had discussed sexual abuse when it was a topic in school, but she never confided in Tasha about any abuse other than verbal.

I didn't like living in the city, so I bought some land outside of Winnipeg and closer to Tasha. One weekend, Tasha called me and asked if she could stay for a week, so she could kick her drug habit. If the drugs weren't readily available, she figured she could give them up. I agreed to let her come. It was the last time she ever stayed with me. She was on an emotional roller coaster for that entire week. One moment she'd be happy, then sad, then angry, then crying. It was hell, and something I said I would never do again. That's why they have Rehab facilities with qualified counselors.

Afterwards, Tasha still smoked pot, as she said she would until she's 80, but I learned to deal with it. After all, it was so much easier than the fighting we did because of the heavier drugs. Or so I thought.

COMPUTER DATING

I'd been on my own for two years. Well, all except for dating a fellow ball player for a bit, but that was nothing serious. Then a co-worker told me about a dating site she'd gone to, so I decided to check it out. They say you have to weed through the garbage to get to the good stuff. This is especially true when it comes to computer dating. I met some real winners, I'll tell you. Some guys were actually married; some had steady girlfriends, while some said they were looking for a relationship, when all they were really after was sex. I also met some really good friends that I still have today.

While all this was going on, I was at least feeling good to be in the country again. I could hear and see the birds, the rabbits, and other wildlife. I could also trudge through the snow anytime I wanted. I had a woodstove and the smell of the smoke from the burning logs was amazing. During the week, the loneliness would kick in, and I would respond by self-medicating with wine. I'd buy the wine on tap in a box, have a couple of glasses in the evening, and chat on the computer. I was fine on the weekends because I spent them with a girlfriend in Winnipeg. I knew I was just existing at the time while using alcohol to cope with my loneliness, but I didn't really care. I felt I wasn't hurting anyone—other than myself.

My girlfriend bought a side-by-side in Winnipeg and asked me if I'd be interested in buying the other half of the house. She wanted a good neighbor, and we spent lots of time together doing things in the city anyway, so why not? Eventually she admitted to me she was scared for me living in the country by myself. I gave in and moved into Winnipeg. Shortly after that, my son Terry moved in with me.

Terry and Douglas were having issues now that Terry was a teenager, so he decided to see how things would go with me. Our agreement was that he would either stay in school, or get a job. If he didn't keep to the plan, he was out. He started off great, but slowly slid downhill. The school had an automated system to inform parents when students didn't attend school. Needless to say, the calls started coming in. Terry didn't like my rules, actually he didn't much like anything except to watch movies all night and sleep all day. I figured he was still a teenager; he'd grow out of it. Evidently he wasn't ready to grow because a few months later, he moved back to Douglas' place.

Meanwhile, I was still meeting new people on the computer, and had begun chatting with a guy named Chad. When I met him, he turned out to be handsome and witty. Plus he treated me like a princess. One month later, he moved in with me and life—at least for a short while—was grand. Chad would sometimes go on business trips for a few days here and there, which allowed us to have our space. I was in love, happy, and feeling like I was on top of the world.

One evening, I was looking on the computer for something and happened to find Chad had set up a new profile on the dating site we met on. I couldn't help but be suspicious. A girlfriend and I set a plan into action to see if Chad was back online looking for someone else. Posing as a potential partner, my girlfriend was able to send me evidence in the form of conversations she had with Chad. I couldn't believe he used the same lines on her that he'd used on me. In his conversations, he told her he was married and in the process of leaving his wife. Chad had actually told me they'd been separated for seven months already. I was sick. For the next two days, I was vomiting and depressed. I couldn't believe I had trusted this guy.

When Chad was scheduled to return from his trip, my girlfriend and I put our sting operation into motion. She made arrangements to pick Chad up at the airport, and I showed up instead. Once confronted, he denied everything. I showed him copies of the conversations he had with my friend and he said he knew (somehow) that I was involved in the conversations.

From the beginning of these developments, I was reporting all the details to my friend next door because she was interested in how it turned out. She had been through something almost identical. She and her husband had separated because he also met a lady online and suddenly started taking business trips out of the blue. Determined to be of some help to me, she set off armed with hard copies of the computer conversations and Chad's home address. It turns out Chad had been indeed married, and was only recently (within the week) separated. His poor wife had no idea he had a new girlfriend, let alone that the two of us were living together.

I was crushed. How stupid could I be? I thought I was on the right path, had grown, and was smarter. I needed to regroup, so I stayed off the computer dating sites for a month. Then the loneliness set in, yet again, and I was back on the dating sites once more.

MICHAEL

Then I met Michael. All the signs were there warning me it was a rebound relationship, but I chose to ignore them. Michael even sent me a letter admitting to his personal struggles, which included depression. He was a long-time student who just graduated from university. It had taken him 10 years to complete a five-year Bachelor of Arts degree due to ongoing breakdowns and depression. Of course I chose to ignore all this because I didn't want to be alone. He made me laugh and feel good about myself, and what was wrong with that? We decided a change of scenery was needed for both of us, and when the opportunity to move to Calgary appeared, we jumped on it.

For the previous five years, I had been at the same job, and had worked my butt off to get where I was. When I asked for an increase in pay I felt I deserved, I was turned down. The company I worked for was Mennonite owned. It was a work culture where women had their place and men were in control. Being turned down for a raise was part of the reason I decided it was time to move on.

Besides, I had always wanted to live in Calgary. In fact, I had headed there when I tried to run away at the age of 15. Now my cousin lived there, and I knew I would have a place to stay if I needed it. So, at the age of 36, with a man I had only known for a few months, I headed to Calgary to start over again

That was May of 2002. We were settling in pretty well. My new job was amazing, and I loved Calgary, but I was having a really hard time supporting the two of us. Michael wasn't working, so he couldn't come through on his promises of, "I'll pay you back! I'll pay you back!" Even basic things like car registration fees were astronomical. Adding to the stress, I couldn't have figured on how much I would miss my children and how much they would miss me. Michael was not only not working; he wasn't even trying very hard to find a job. Yet he somehow managed to line up a second job for me. As happy as I was, he was depressed. With all the financial stress and many hours I was putting into work, our relationship was falling apart. One evening, my boss from the second job came over to discuss a financial plan. Instead of being part of the discussion, Michael stayed in the bedroom crying and claiming he couldn't face anybody, so he asked me to look after things. I knew at that moment our relationship was over.

I ended up buying Michael a one-way plane ticket to Victoria, B.C., helped him pack his belongings, lined up a truck to move them, and sent him on his way. A week later he called me, said he couldn't afford to pay for the moving truck, had nowhere to store his stuff, and wanted me to look after the moving costs. I told him his belongings were on the truck heading towards Victoria, so he better figure things out. A week later he had a job making $10 an hour. Funny, he wouldn't work in Calgary unless he was making at least $20 an hour. But that was when he had someone else to foot the bills.

In spite of being in another dead-end relationship, there were some lessons learned. Michael was an artist. He took me to galleries and taught me how to appreciate art. Among other changes, I updated my wardrobe to the 90's. I felt like a new woman. I went from country girl to an IKEA lady with more class. Bye bye farm girl.

BACK TO SCHOOL

In October of 2002, I returned to Winnipeg and my children. I had a huge debt load, and had to start over, yet again. I asked my parents to help me financially, and they did—with restrictions. They gave me a small loan to cover my debt with payment arrangements and interest charges.

Sitting in the bank lobby, while my parents and their financial advisor discussed my financial future was one of the most embarrassing situations I've ever been in. There I was, 36 years old, sitting in my hometown bank, waiting for my parents to decide whether or not they would even help me. In my mind, the 16 years of slave labor they received from me at $3 per week allowance was more than enough payment, and they should have just given me the money. But they didn't see it that way.

After all, they were partially in this cushy financial position because of the cheap labor they'd had when they started the farm. Cheap child labor, mainly mine, that is! Rumors around town indicated my parents sued a company for a car accident we were in when I was 16. A lot of the case was based on my being pregnant at the time. Did I ever see, or even hear anything about this? No. Not a word from my parents, anyway. It was my ex-in laws who eventually told me about it.

My parents didn't want me to know how much they were worth, or where the money they were going to loan me was coming from, so they left me out in the waiting room, waiting to hear my fate. My brother once told me my parents owned everything on the farm. I had no idea. He said they were worth a couple of million dollars. That was quite a few years prior to this scenario. Whatever their situation, they were able to back my brother when he set up his farm, as well as my sister to set up her pharmacy—so my small amount shouldn't create that big of a stir in their financial pot.

Now that I look back, I should have filed for bankruptcy at that time. This would have allowed me to avoid the whole scene in the bank and the financial hold they gained over me. However, my bills got paid, and I started to settle in again. Now it was time to rebuild my relationship with Tasha.

During my stay in Calgary, Tasha was involved with the wrong people. She was using cocaine as well as several other illegal drugs, and ended up with a drug trafficking charge. I arrived home in time to take her to the hospital for a blood transfusion due to overuse of Depo-Provera (the birth control shot). I told her she should sue her doctor for leaving her on it for four years. All medical information advises two years at the most. Tasha was back out of the hospital, and then faced court appearances for her charge. She went through a rough patch cutting ties with her boyfriend and kicking the habit again. I supported her as much as I could.

On returning to Winnipeg, I had moved into a two bedroom duplex with an old coworker. I also went back to school for Human Resource Management. Life was actually pretty good. I was managing things well. I was happy with school and with my grades. I was overall happy in life. I decided it might be a good time to try computer dating again.

The first guy I met and dated was Kerry. After two months, I realized he was just as controlling as the other men I had gone out with. At least this time I recognized it before too much time had passed or, God forbid, I might have moved in with him. A weekend at my sister's with her controlling husband butting heads with my controlling boyfriend did not go over very well at all, but it showed me who I was dealing with.

After that relationship fizzled out, I realized again that I had learned a lot about myself, and more about the standards I wanted. I also wrote a bit of poetry. Here are two poems from that period.

The Journey

She stands alone in front of the mountain.
The journey was long,
the road not forgotten.

She turns her head
looks over her shoulder.
No one is there,
no one has followed.

She sees the path that she has chosen.
Choices she made that led her here.
People she met,
their names forgotten.

Her hair is long and grey in color.
She's older now,
Yet younger than her years.

The Meadow she just left,
Is full of beautiful flowers,
White and blue.
Pure and sweet their fragrance fills the air.

She remembers walking through.

Hands gliding over the long grass,
Bending to smell the flowers.

Off in the far distance she can barely see,
The forest she once walked through.

She turns back to look at the Mountain
She's climbed it before.
Oddly though there is no fear.
Calm and tranquil,
Soft and tender.
She admires the strength of the Mountain.

At the base where she stands are trees and rock
Half way up she sees outcroppings and caves
At the peak, beautiful white snow
She is not scared,
Even though she stands alone.

The sun warms her back,
Her body glows.
She knows who she is.
Her essence emulates,
Through every pore of her being.

She sees a path winding up the mountain

Her first step in a new direction.
For this one is different.
This one she follows the path,
Not climbs the rock.
The journey continues on,
Even as she walks alone.

... Lisa M. Sobry

What is love?

What is love?
I do not know.

A smile or a touch that makes me cry.
Or is it a sigh as he walks by?

The touch of a hand, the taste of a kiss.
Is it someone I should miss?

Softness and gentleness, kindness and care.
Is that what we're supposed to share?

The wink of an eye, that little glow.
Do you move very slow?

Laughter and joy fill your heart.
Is it really like a tart?

Sweet and sugary full of spice.
Should it really be that nice?

The earth moves, the fire explodes.
Why is it all written in codes?

Some day I'm sure I will see.
What love is actually supposed to be.

... Lisa M. Sobry

During the short relationship with Kerry, I moved into an apartment and felt my sense of freedom and self return. Meanwhile, I could see his control with his daughter and how it was starting to affect me. My cousin from Calgary and I spoke on many occasions. She was an amazing confidant, helping me work through some of my issues. Each time I said I wanted to break it off with Kerry, she reminded me it was "that time of the month," which was usually the time I wanted to end a relationship. So I continued seeing him for another month just to make sure. I finally ended it shortly after that, just around the time Kerry was due to go on a vacation. He went, but came back early, and called me a week later to get together. Too late. In my mind, the relationship was over before he left on his trip.

Terry came to live with me after that. I told him if he lived with me, he'd have to work. He promised to get a job, so I moved into a two bedroom apartment big enough for the two of us. He did get a job, so I let him stay. Then a buddy of his was kicked out of his house, so he came to stay with us. Then Tasha was having issues at her residence, so she moved in as well. Terry's job didn't last very long, and all hell broke loose. The agreement was he worked, or out he went. Terry no longer had a job, so, out he went. In the end, I called the crisis centre, and he spent a few days in a shelter. Tough Love, remember? Tough on the children, but extremely tough on the parents, too. Watching your children struggle and trying to keep your boundaries is one of the most difficult things a parent can do. I had many restless nights worrying about him in a place like that. Tears of joy often came when I would see him, and see for myself that he was okay. I loved him so much, but he needed to learn his own lessons on his own.

My parents were hounding me for payments on the money I borrowed, and because Terry was no longer contributing financially, things were getting tighter and tighter. The apartment felt crowded, and I was starting to slide back into depression again.

Looking for some relief, I'd returned to computer dating again. That's when I met Marcel online. We'd been talking for a while before I met him. Soon we started spending time together, and developing a friendship.

In August, I finished school and got my diploma in Human Resource Management. I started applying for jobs. One of the jobs I was looking at was in Portage la Prairie where Marcel lived. He'd been thinking of getting a roommate, so when a position was offered to me, I accepted it. It was time for me to live my life and let my grown children live theirs. I decided to leave Winnipeg again, but I didn't leave my kids stranded. I left them my furniture, dishes, and most of my belongings. They took over the lease at the apartment and so my new journey began.

MARCEL

Marcel and I started dating in November of 2003 and were together for four years. I found it very difficult living with someone again, starting a new job, and moving to a new community. After a couple of months, I went back on antidepressant medication to straighten out my serotonin levels. I was falling back into the pit of depression, which in the past had led to a nervous breakdown. I was not going to allow that to happen. But even with the medication, I was still struggling. I was crying a lot, having difficulty with a coworker, and thinking I'd made a mistake moving. Tasha and I got into a huge argument over money and a car she totalled, so we weren't speaking to each other.

Adding to my stress, I found out Marcel was talking on MSN with a woman he had wanted to date prior to meeting me. He was flirting with her online. Because of the incident with Chad, I had trust issues I needed to deal with.

Marcel was also on antidepressant medication. As with other new men in my life, the warning signs were there, but I ignored them. We had some major arguments over my insecurities about the MSN "chat woman" and his refusal to stop flirting with her. Eventually I made him choose. Even though he chose me, it wasn't enough to calm my fears, or fix things.

I was talking on MSN to one of my kids early one morning when Marcel came on. He assumed I was online at that time to check up on him. In retaliation, he started talking to his chat woman again. We fought and I moved into the spare bedroom. I seriously thought about moving out. How could I be with someone who, out of spite, prolonged such a mess? I was really struggling, trying to decide what to do. I confided in a girlfriend, and then I made the mistake of telling Marcel that I had shared my struggles her. I made the bigger mistake of relaying to him her comments regarding him and our relationship. This created more stress, but we worked through it. At least we were communicating and getting closer as a couple. I was applying the lessons I had learned from previous failed relationships, and thought I knew what I was doing. It seemed we both just needed to re-adjust to being in a relationship and living with another person.

Then we started talking about moving closer to Winnipeg. Marcel was serious about leaving his job of 23 years. I found a job in Winnipeg and in order to get established there, I stayed with the same girlfriend I had confided in. Marcel felt very uncomfortable with this setup because of her previous comments about him. She also didn't think much of his family. So, it turned out I didn't stay with her very long.

During this period, I started working out with Marcel's sister at the local YMCA. We had interesting conversations, which gave me insight into Marcel, but I learned very quickly how opinionated she was. I also observed the amount of control she had over the rest of her family. I'd learned from friends in the past to keep your friends close and your enemies even closer. Due to the level of interference at this early stage of our relationship, I knew it would only get worse as time went on. Marcel had also warned me not to get too close to his family.

One day, I received tragic news. Tasha called to report Douglas had been shot and she was on her way to the hospital. She then learned he had died in the ambulance en route. I was numb and unsure of what to do. My relationship with my closest girlfriend was now strained, so I confided in Marcel's sister. At the time it seemed like a good idea, but I would soon find out how judgmental his sister really was.

Marcel was very supportive through this situation. Even when Douglas' mother was yelling at me over the phone, telling me she didn't want me at the funeral,

Marcel offered comfort. I spoke with both Tasha and Terry and they wanted me there. For their sake, I went to the funeral. Plus I just wanted to pay my respects. Even though Douglas and I did not see eye to eye, he was the father of my children. As family members, he and my children deserved respect from me. What I didn't expect was that after the funeral, Tasha and I started talking again. And Terry, Anna, and I became closer.

Because my living arrangements changed again, I was now commuting every day into Winnipeg. My position was only casual. When it was cut to only one day a week, another job opportunity presented itself, and I accepted it. Marcel and I discussed moving again and looked at a few acreages outside the city, but they didn't suit Marcel's ideals of where he wanted to live. I'd been working at the new position for five months when it became obvious Marcel was not going to move. I wasn't going to commute for eleven years until he retired, so I left my job.

More financial stressed followed. In the end, I was forced to declare bankruptcy. Marcel felt he shouldn't have to pay anything toward my debt because I had accumulated it. I felt useless, depressed, and overwhelmed with life itself.

One benefit of the bankruptcy was at least my debt was completely gone. All except for the loan my parents gave me, that is. They wanted their money back which, of course, I didn't have. How did my parents expect me to pay them back when I had no income? I couldn't even afford my car payments and eventually gave my car back.

I virtually went into hiding. I spent the summer with Anna and Marcel camping and just hanging out. One thing I'm grateful for during that period is that Anna and I had quality time together.

That fall, I decided to go back into the hairdressing industry. I'd kept my skills up over the years, so I still knew what I was doing. My first job lasted a month; the owner of the shop I worked at was very controlling, and the gossip there was unreal. I did, however, learn some new techniques from the younger stylists working in the establishment. After leaving, I became a self-employed hairstylist in another shop.

My clientele was slowly building, but I was having issues again with the owner of this shop. Many of my clients had been, or currently were her clients, and I wasn't doing exactly what she did, so they were complaining about my work. I should have known better, working with Mennonite clientele. My experience with Mennonites in Steinbach had taught me many are critical or judgemental towards outsiders. You'd think I would have learned my lesson by now, but I hadn't known the clienteles' backgrounds before I started working. I felt insecure about my work, and fell back into the trying-to-please-mode I had with my parents.

I also worked for a few months as a manager for a portrait studio in a huge conglomerate store. This gave me time to build up my hairstyling clientele as well as learn skills to help Marcel with his photography. A lady there, Kathy, was going on maternity leave and I would have a few months to learn my role as a manager. Then, Kathy went on sick leave nine days after I started, leaving me with a full-time job and no employees to help. I talked to my District Manager and got permission to hire an assistant. Unfortunately, I made the mistake of hiring an employee whom Kathy didn't like.

Kathy wasn't happy about this situation, so she undermined everything I did. She called the Regional Manager, removed our information book, took a computer monitor, and removed client portraits off the wall. All of these instances happened after hours, or when I wasn't working. As I continued struggling trying to do my job, while trying not to become a victim of the conglomerate store gossip pit, I noticed some discrepancies in financial records. My District Manager and I started investigating, and allegations were made against Kathy. To make a long story short, the Regional and Canadian Managers had been through this once before and did not want to have a second manager fired due to theft of money, so they covered it up. They offered the District Manager a choice: Take a buyout, or they would get rid of her. The corporate bosses thought the she had been morally obligated to report Kathy's theft to the RCMP. She knew if she stayed, she would not be able to stay quiet about the situation and it would lead to her termination of employment, so she took the buyout. I refused to work for a company who would use such underhanded techniques. I couldn't believe they would even think of taking Kathy back after everything that happened.

The lesson I learned here was to trust my instincts. When I first received a phone call from Kathy, I turned down an interview with her because of how I felt during the conversation. After long discussions with Marcel, however, we decided it might be a good opportunity for both of us. At one point, I suggested he take the job as it was in his field, but the salary was way too low for him. I decided I could do it, so I phoned Kathy back and she hired me on the spot. I later found out I was the only person who applied for the position. I should have trusted my instincts when I first talked to her.

Marcel and I continued to struggle. Many of our troubles stemmed from issues in past relationships that we needed to deal with. But we also kept having financial problems. We often felt like the other person was out to get us, not supporting us, and misinterpreting our conversations. *Snowballing* is the term Marcel and I used. That's when you take a piece of information, overanalyze it—mull it over and over again—until it becomes like a snowball rolling down a hill. It just keeps getting bigger and eventually careens out of control.

Luckily, we were committed to getting outside help for our conflict. Our counselor helped us through the communication part. Marcel's family was interfering in our relationship at the time. Plus they had a huge family secret they were keeping from a sibling. This was creating undue stress on Marcel that, in turn, affected our relationship. That, on top of our ongoing financial stress. Although we were communicating better and arguing less, we still weren't moving forward.

One thing that started to become clear for me was that our understanding of commitment in a relationship differed. He thought commitment meant simply living together. I thought commitment was symbolized with an engagement ring and meant sharing and building a life together.

On the surface, we looked like a committed couple. We shared everything—everything was his and mine together in the same house. We owned a DVD player together and had the couples share plan on our cell phones and that was it. After four years, I felt this wasn't the level of commitment I wanted. I tried explaining how women and men see commitment differently. I was so frustrated that I couldn't get him to understand me. Meanwhile, my parents announcing their plan to visit us during that period didn't help our stress levels any either.

MY MOTHER

In September 2006, my parents stopped in for a visit. I showed my mother my business in the basement. The spare bedroom was changed into my space. I offered Reiki sessions, card readings and meditation services and had essential oils and a few crystals for retail sale. She laughed for five minutes straight, then apologized and said, "It's all hocus-pocus, don't you think?"

All I could think about at that moment was why she never stopped my father from abusing me, so I asked her. She said she never believed me and couldn't believe my father would do such a thing. I asked her about my brothers and if my oldest brother were to have children, would she protect them. Wouldn't she be scared of what might happen to them given his history with my kids? My mother told me if that did happen, it would be between his wife and him. I asked if, as a grandmother, she would protect her own grandchildren. She said again, anything that happened would be between him and his wife.

She then turned the tables and asked me if my daughter was still doing drugs. I asked her why she wanted to know—was it out of concern for her granddaughter, or was it a chance to get back at me. She said it was my fault Tasha was the way she was because I was a single mom and because of the life I had led. I said, "Don't you think it might be because your sons molested her!" She said that they were just boys doing boy things.

At that moment, I finally got it. I did not want to be associated with my parents, or brother ever again. The choices they made were not healthy for me, or for the intention of going after what was the greatest good for me. Besides, I would never be able to reach the expectations my mother had set for me.

I only went to my parents' 40th wedding anniversary the next month because I didn't want to leave all the responsibilities on my sister's shoulders. I had agreed to help her months before, and I kept my word. I haven't seen or talked to my parents since that time. My mother emailed me a few times, but I never replied.

Marcel and I spoke at great length regarding my parents and my past. He knew what happened. He supported me in any decision I made regarding my parents, and agreed the anxiety I felt prior to any visits with my parents was unbearable. He couldn't understand how a father could do that to a child, how a mother wouldn't stop it, or how parents who were financially wealthy would sit back and not help their struggling daughter. They had once even asked Marcel to pay off my loan, and he flat out refused. I was grateful that Marcel supported my decision not to have anything to do with them anymore.

I couldn't believe I was cutting off ties with my parents. What a relief! I felt like this huge burden had been lifted off my shoulders and I was finally free. Finally! I wish I'd done this when I was 20 years old. That way my children would have been protected. However, I believe everything happens for a reason. I believe the lessons learned from one situation—especially the hard ones—are used in all other areas of our lives. All of our experiences and lessons make us who we are today.

SERENITY OASIS

The gossip in the hairdressing shop was getting worse and I was struggling to maintain a positive outlook on life. Marcel and I were still in counseling trying to make our relationship work. I accepted a position in Winnipeg working part-time in a spiritual store for the Christmas rush and figured whatever is meant to be, will be. I drove into Winnipeg and stayed in a girlfriend's basement. Because she had four cats, I set up a tent and had my own room.

This gave Marcel and me a few days apart during the week and I was hoping it would help our relationship. It did in the beginning, but the tranquility was short lived as new owners were taking over the business, and I was starting my own.

Tasha introduced me to prayer beads, and I started using them daily. "I am a successful business woman," repeated 108 times every night before I went to bed. Two weeks later a position presented itself for me to start a Holistic Business, and I did. Serenity Oasis opened on December 23, 2006. I chose the name Serenity Oasis back in 1999 when I first started my spiritual journey. At that time, I had come up with this brilliant plan to build a five-acre, enclosed oasis with a serene environment. My hope was that anyone entering the establishment would automatically feel the serenity as they walked through the doors. With the installment of water fountains, bridges, orchards, and gardens an oasis was formed. Although the end result is a much smaller version of the original I had in mind, the basic principles still apply. The healing energy, serene environment, and peaceful outdoor gardens have brought to life a vision I had eight years ago.

The following excerpt is from the local paper:

> The doors are open and the universe is invited to visit a new and unique business. The air is slightly tinged with the aroma of essential oil bath salts and soaps. Relaxation music wafts throughout the building. A feeling of calm and peace fills the soul as the world is left behind the closed door.
>
> For several years, owner Lisa Sobry has felt the world is too full of stress. "We put expectations and limitations on ourselves thus creating physical ailments

> to our bodies and mental anguish to our minds," she says.
>
> Serenity Oasis was created to help people feel better about themselves, to feel more secure about who they are and where they want to be in their lives.
>
> Relax your mind with meditation. Treat your body to a facial, body-scrub, or nail service accompanied with a new hairstyle. Detoxify your body with reflexology. Lift your spirit through Reiki, or chakra clearing.
>
> Come see a unique selection of gifts- Himalayan salt, crystals, gem stones, bath salts, candles, jewelry, fairies, books, photographs, and much more.

It was all that, and more. However, in the end, it cost me my relationship with Marcel. His sister continued inputting her two cents into our relationship. Finances remained tight at home. Marcel was helping me a great deal with the business, even though he was struggling at his own work. Finally, he had a nervous breakdown.

There I was, trying to establish a new business, while trying to help him, while trying not to lose the spirituality I'd gained. I didn't want to be forced to affirm my beliefs to defend myself. So, I ended up moving out.

Currently we have our own space and we are still growing as individuals. Somewhere along the way while living together, we lost our individuality. I knew regaining it would make us stronger and happier people.

As a business owner, I've had trials and tribulations, but all are taken in stride. All are taken one day at a time. My business provides tools to those wishing to move forward in their lives. I offer them because they are tools that have worked for me. With them, I've opened myself tremendously to develop my spiritual potential. I believe that is why I'm here today.

I'm proud to say that Serenity Oasis provides services in meditation, qigong, massage, and so many other modalities, along with a New Age retail store. In addition, I offer spiritual guidance.

Even though at the beginning of my spiritual journey, I kept coming and going off my spiritual path, I kept coming back to it. I know I struggled during those periods more than I needed to, but the lessons learned, both on that path and when I strayed away from it, are what have brought me to where I am today.

WHAT I'VE LEARNED

I firmly believe everything happens for a reason, and the reason I have found for my survival is writing this book and letting other survivors know they are not alone.

After reviewing my story several times, I've found that yes, I've had many romantic relationships. Now I understand why. I needed a protector in my life. I needed someone to watch over me just in case an abusive situation would arise. Who would protect me? Who would protect my children? I, myself, had failed on both counts.

Another thing I noticed in my relationships was that my partners often had a controlling female in their lives. Whether it was a mother, or sister, such women were somewhere in the picture, giving unwanted advice, planting seeds of doubt in my partner's mind, or basically sticking their nose in where it didn't belong. This control eventually overshadowed my partner's sense of control, so they imposed their own need for control in our relationship, thus creating a power struggle. Defenses would go up on both sides and that's when the relationship would begin to slide downhill.

Now, if you asked any of my former partners, they would probably deny this because they wouldn't see the outside control being forced on them. Denial is the way we cope with issues we don't understand. It is a psychological defense mechanism in which a person faced with a fact that is uncomfortable or too painful to accept, rejects it. Instead, the person insists that it is not true despite overwhelming evidence to the contrary.

If you apply the concept of denial to my story, you will first see denial from my mother, then from my sister, teachers, personal and social relationships, and lastly and more importantly, from me. Most of the characters in my story do not want to know how to be responsible for their actions, and don't care who they hurt. I, on the other hand, am trying to claim responsibility, so I can grow even stronger.

I've come a long way as a human being, and that is partly because I take responsibility for my actions. Although my story may give the impression that I'm blaming others with, "It's all their fault," nothing could be further from the truth. Sure, I've had my share of anger issues, which I've had to work through. I have ongoing self-confidence and self-esteem issues that still nag at me today. And some fears continue to haunt me. How many 40-year-old women do you know who still change their clothes in the dark, just in case someone might walk in on them—even when they live by themselves?!

I've learned that my body is often a barometer that lets me know how well I'm dealing with my stress levels. For example, my weight still fluctuates up and down depending on what's going on and how well I'm dealing with things.

I don't know if I will ever work through all my issues; however, I do know I'm going to try my best to work through as many as I can. If that means more counseling for me in the future, then so be it. I understand that this is a life-long journey.

Counseling can help you move forward in your life. It should also help you learn how to be strong to stand on your own. The more you work through your issues, the stronger you can become. Don't put up with any kind of harassment in the workplace, at home, or by outside influential people anymore. Learn how to be strong, and learn how to stand up for yourself.

Counseling can be a wonderful way to get people to open their eyes, but only if they are ready. And forcing someone else to go for counseling does not work. The best you can do is to start to work on yourself, and hope the other people in your life in need of some self-awareness will follow your lead.

A word of caution: Make sure you choose a counselor who is right for you. If you don't feel comfortable with your counselor, find another one. You have your particular issues, and you need the right person to help you deal with them. Look for a person you can trust, a person you feel good being around, and who will guide you in the best direction for your life. The best guidance for you is guidance that helps you grow in healthy ways.

The Appendix section of this book lists information to help you contact the Human Rights Commission, Teen Hotline, Crisis Centre, Women's Shelter, and several other Canadian resources. (If you live in another country, the internet will list many resources in your community or available online.)

If you are being abused, trusting the abuser, whether a mother who didn't protect you, siblings you would never think could do such a thing, a father, partners, husbands, boyfriends, girlfriends, grandparents, friends, or cousins, is not in your best interests. An abuser will abuse, molest, or rape anyone the first chance they get.

If you are being abused, tell someone. Tell your parents, grandparents, your best friend, sister, brother, teacher, principal, guidance counselor, your next door neighbor, ANYBODY. Tell as many as people you need to, until somebody listens. If you can't talk about it, write about it.

The most important thing I've learned throughout my life is: *No one sticks up for you except you, so stand tall and be strong.* Dependable friends, partners, and lovers will be there, but the only person who can fill the void within you is you. Once you learn how to fill the void within yourself, you will never have to count on anyone else to make you happy, or to show you the pleasures and gifts this beautiful planet has to offer.

You will be able to count on yourself to show you the way, to direct you on the path that should be chosen, to trust the people you should trust, and to know deep down inside that you are loved, you belong here, and you are a special person.

In closing, I hope that my story has provided you with tools you can use to survive and thrive. The greatest gift I can give you is from what I've learned myself: Respect yourself and love yourself. Ultimately, you must give yourself this gift in order to grow. By sharing my journey, I hope that I have encouraged you on your journey. I also hope you didn't need too many tissues!

As I sit here today, I can't help but note that it is 07-07-2007, a fitting day to end my first book due to its spiritual and metaphysical qualities. *Metaphysical* means that which is beyond what can be grasped by the senses. It is a Greek term that comes from Aristotle, when he was talking about some form of theological philosophy. It means something else in today's world, however. It refers to that which underlies everything, of which spirits are a part. Spirits seeking wholeness. Like yours and mine.

I recently came across a poem I had written years back. Its ending provides a perfect ending to this story. It reminds me that I not only survived the abuse I endured, but thanks to my spiritual journey, I also learned to thrive. Here's an excerpt from my poem *Personal Growth*:

> ... Years of hatred finally set free.
> Pain is but a memory
> Tucked away in her mind
> A chapter in her life that wasn't very kind.
>
> Now she knew what they did not.
> She is beautiful, yes she is.
> Inside where they cannot see
> Deep within, in a perfect spot
>
> Soft and gentle,
> Full of love.
> She gave the gift of life to three
> With hopes they would always be free.

As she grows
Some may see
Light and love flow from her soul.
Happiness and joy fill her heart.
Spread a smile she says,
That's a good start.

Tears of joy run down her face,
As she smiles at the image of the woman
She knew she could be.
Elegant and beautiful
She stands so tall.
One would never know
She had felt so very small.

...Lisa M. Sobry

RESOURCES

Canadian Mental Health Association
Provides contact information for counsellors across the country. If you are having mental difficulties with your divorce, arguing with your spouse, or facing constant outbursts from your children, contact your nearest branch. They will help you and your children. You can also ask your doctor for a referral.
Web: *www.cmha.ca*

Children's Advocate
Children have the right to be heard and be a part of decisions you are making in child visitation. If children or parents feel this is not happening, they may contact the advocacy.
Phone: 204-988-7440
Toll Free: 1-800-263-7146
Web: *www.childrensadvocate.mb.ca/who-are-we*

Child and Family Services
Children have the right to be safe regardless of which parent they are with. Mental, verbal, physical, and sexual abuse issues are handled through this agency. Protect your child especially if there is a history of violence with your ex-spouse.
Web: *www.gov.mb.ca/fs/childfam*

Child Welfare Information Gateway
This website provides web and phone contact information for each State.
Web:
https://www.childwelfare.gov/pubs/reslist/rl_dsp.cfm?rs_id=5&rate_chno=11-11172

cybertip!ca
Toll Free: 1-866-658-9022
Web: *www.cybertip.ca*

Families Anonymous
Winnipeg, MB
Phone: (204) 237-0336 / World Service (310) 815-8010
Web: *www.FamiliesAnonymous.org*

Klinic Community Health Centre
Offers free counselling to men, women, transgendered people, and children. They have a drop-in counselling service which allows for immediate help.
Phone: 204-784-4090
Web: *www.klinic.mb.ca/counsellingservices.htm*

Men's Resource Centre
The centre provides free counselling and support to men, on a range of issues, in a manner that feels comfortable and familiar to men.
Phone: 204-415-6797
Toll Free: 1-855-672-6727
Web: *http://www.mens-resource-centre.ca*

National Child Abuse Hotline
Phone: 1-800-422-4453
Web: *http://www.childhelp.org/pages/hotline-home*

National Domestic Violence Hotline
Toll Free: 1-800-799-7233
Web: *http://www.thehotline.org/*

National Hotline for Missing & Exploited Children
Toll Free: 1-800-843-5678

Web: *missingkids.com*
National Runaway Hotline
Toll Free: 1-800-786-2929
Web: *runaway.org*

Rainbows
This program is offered through school counsellors. It provides a basic outline for parents divorcing and how to help their children cope with changes in the family.
Web: *www.rainbows.ca*

Safe Horizon
Toll free: 1-800-621-4673
Web: *http://www.safehorizon.org/index/get-help-8.html*

Fort Garry Women's Resource Centre
Phone: 204-477-1123
Web: *www.fgwrc.ca*

Interlake Women's Resource Centre
Phone: 204-642-8264
Web: *www.interlakewomen.ca*

Lakeshore Women's Resource Centre
Phone: 204-768-3016
Web: *lwrc.weebly.com/index*

Maggie's Resource Centre
Phone: 613-332-3010
Web: *www.maggiesresource.com*

Ontario Association of Women's Centres
Web: *www.oawc.org*

The Women's Resource Centre
Phone: (204) 726-8632
Web: *thewomenscentrebrandon.com*

Manitoba Association of Women's Shelters
Toll Free: 1-877-977-0007 (24/7 crisis line)
Web: *maws.mb.ca*

ABOUT THE AUTHOR

Lisa M. Sobry is a certified Life Coach, Past Life Regressionist, Reiki Master, Medium, Angel Card Reader and Modern Mystery School Initiate. She facilitates workshops and retreats, and speaks publicly throughout North America about her writing and abuse.

If you would like more information about Lisa M. Sobry's workshops, retreats, books, or CDs, you may visit her at:

Website: *www.lisasobry.com*
Email: *lisasobry@hotmail.com*

OTHER BOOKS WRITTEN BY LISA M. SOBRY

Awakening!
Enduring
New Beginnings
Divorcing Amy
I Survived So Can You
Who I Truly Am
Finding My Way - Opening To Mediumship

CDS BY LISA M. SOBRY

Self-Empowerment "A Guided Journey to the Mountains"

Made in the USA
Charleston, SC
14 April 2014